FOR THE LOVE OF
LEMURS

Praise for *For the Love of Lemurs*

"Pat's story took me on an inspirational journey that will remain with me forever. Truly."—**Morgan Freeman**, actor

"What a delight to have so many of Pat Wright's adventures in Madagascar in one book. I have been following her work for 30 years now, and what she has accomplished there is simply miraculous. Pat is a true eco hero, one of the best ever, and her program in Ranomafana is a model for conservationists everywhere."
—**Russ Mittermeier**, president, Conservation International and chairman, IUCN/SSC Primate Specialist Group

"A static summary of achievements is not enough to convey Pat's impact on protecting lemurs and their habitat in Madagascar."
—**Michael Crowther**, president and CEO of the Indianapolis Zoological Society

"She found the greater bamboo lemur, which everyone thought had been extinct for 50 years. She discovered the golden bamboo lemur, which nobody had ever even seen before. Pat is a real hero. For her, conservation isn't just about animals, it's about all the people that live around the animals, and making everybody's lives better."
—**Drew Fellman**, Producer and Writer, *Island of Lemurs*

FOR THE LOVE OF
LEMURS

MY LIFE IN THE WILDS
OF MADAGASCAR

Patricia Chapple Wright

LANTERN BOOKS | NEW YORK
A Division of Booklight Inc.

2016
Lantern Books
128 2nd Place
Brooklyn, NY 11231-4102
www.lanternbooks.com

Printed in the United States of America

Library of Congress cataloging-in-publication data is available.
Wright, Patricia C., 1944–
For the love of lemurs : my life in the wilds of Madagascar /
Patricia Chapple Wright.
pages cm
ISBN 978-1-59056-445-5 (hardcover : alk. paper)
ISBN 978-1-59056-547-6
ISBN 978-1-59056-446-2 (ebook)
1. Lemurs—Madagascar. 2. Wright, Patricia C., 1944–
3. Ranomafana National Park (Madagascar) I. Title.
QL737.P95W75 2014
599.8'3—dc23
2014029559

To Elwyn LaVerne Simons,
for encouraging me to go to Madagascar

To Benjamin Andriamihaja,
without whom all this would not have been possible

To my grandchildren, Arianna and Issan Poston,
who give me hope for the future

CONTENTS

Contents

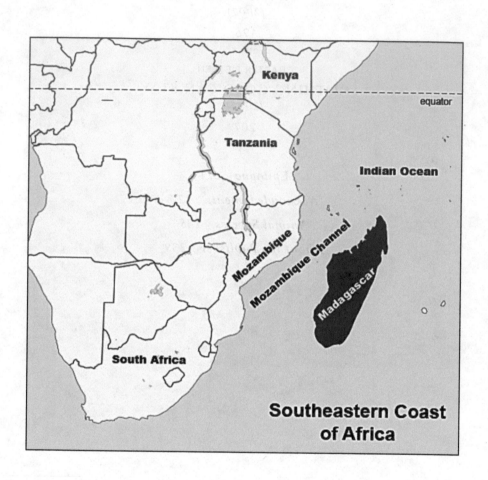

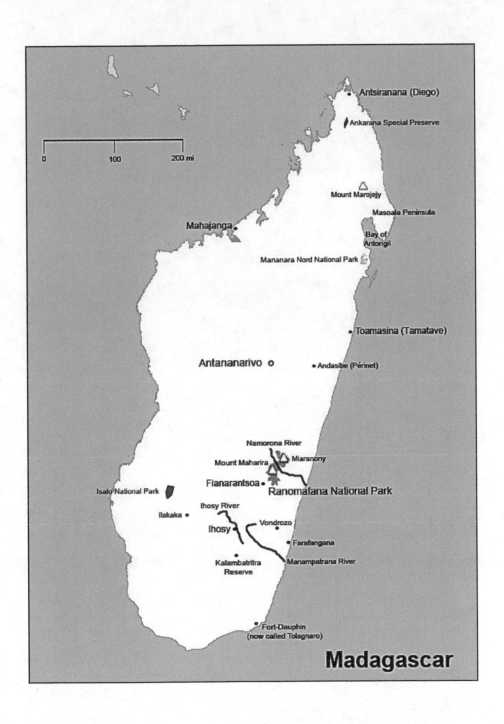

Madagascar

CHAPTER ONE

GOLD RUSH

(1986)

IT WAS PITCH BLACK in the large room at Duke University Primate Center, as I watched the tiny tarsier with my red filtered light. Amos was perched in a tree in the center of the room, his huge eyes able to see in the dark. I had brought this male back from the Philippines as part of my study of tarsier behavior. Amos gave a shrill, loud whistle and Mindanao in the next room snapped her head around, and flicked her ears toward the call. The doors between the two rooms were open, but Chani, in a third room, was also twitching her ears toward the call. Both females began to leap through their open doors in the direction of Amos' whistle. Would the two females fight over him? I held my breath.

Just then my pager buzzed, signaling that my boss, Professor Elwyn Simons, wanted me to come upstairs to his office. Startled by the sharp buzz, the female tarsiers raced back to their rooms and I closed the doors. Elwyn, a world-renowned fossil hunter, was the director of the Primate Center. I finished my research notes for this session and walked upstairs to find out the urgent news.

"Wright," Elwyn said the moment I entered his office. "We have a problem. There's a lemur in Madagascar that we suspect is extinct—*Hapalemur simus*, the greater bamboo lemur. I would like you to find this lemur . . . *alive*." He shouted the last word for emphasis. Elwyn was not a tall man, but he had a way of expanding his presence. His features reminded me of Ernest Hemingway's, and his single-mindedness was apparent.

"Here, look at this painting from the 1800s." He pointed to a framed picture on the wall, which depicted a squirrel-like creature with a moss-gray body and subtle white ear tufts. *Rather drab*, I thought.

"Fewer than five hundred years ago, giant lemurs lived throughout Madagascar, some as big as a gorilla. The greater bamboo lemur was one of them. We find its bones everywhere in the north of Madagascar, in the limestone karst caves, the western canyons, the marshes of the central plateau: locations that are hundreds and hundreds of miles apart."

Elwyn then pointed at the rows of skulls, jaws, and leg and arm bones of subfossil[1] giant lemurs displayed on his shelves, the fruits of his paleontological labors after years of field work in Madagascar. Some bones had cut marks on them, indicating they'd been butchered by humans. When the first people

---

1 *Subfossil* refers to material that hasn't yet fully fossilized because it's too recent or the conditions where the matter was found aren't fully suitable for fossilization.

arrived in Madagascar around two thousand years ago, the giant lemurs were probably easy prey. It would take another thousand years, however, before hunting began to threaten them with extinction.

I stared at the empty eye sockets of the skulls of all those lost species. "But now?"

"The greater bamboo lemur is the smallest of them and the only one of the species of subfossil lemur that's left. It was first described by explorers in 1851. Some were captured and kept in captivity, but they didn't live long. A group was seen in the southeastern rainforest decades ago. In 1955, Professor Jean-Jacques Petter saw a dead one in a cooking pot farther south, in a town called Vondrozo. Another group was seen lurking about a coffee plantation at dusk. But those sightings were long ago."

Elwyn snapped his eyes onto mine. "Wright. Can you find it? Can you be the first in modern history to find the greater bamboo lemur alive?"

He was issuing me a direct challenge, as he had done before. Three years previously, Elwyn had brought me to the Duke Primate Center in North Carolina. I was a graduate student at City University of New York, fresh from spending years in the Amazon rainforest studying the secretive habits of *Aotus*, the owl monkey. I had begun my career as a social worker and Brooklyn housewife, but had become obsessed by a monkey I purchased in a New York pet store. Questions about this monkey's behavior had led me to the South American rainforests, dragging my artist-painter husband and my three-year-old daughter along with me. The result was the first paper written on wild night monkeys. After entering graduate school, and now a single mom, I had taken Amanda into the remotest of field sites with a team of biologists as I conducted my research on the evolution of how male *Aotus* looked after their young. (I write about these adventures in my first book, *High Moon Over the Amazon*.)

Even before I'd finished writing my dissertation, Elwyn had called and offered me a job at Duke. My first assignment had been to track down and capture tarsiers, a tiny nocturnal primate, for study in captivity, something no one had been able to accomplish before. I had traveled to Borneo and the Philippines and had returned with twenty-four tarsiers of two species. I'd been studying their behavior and infant development ever since.

Elwyn had hired me because we were kindred spirits. We both appreciated a challenge. He loved extinct primates; I loved extant ones. The notion that an extinct lemur was in fact alive and still undiscovered seemed far-fetched to me. But Elwyn had already been awarded a National Science Foundation grant to look for this supposedly extinct animal, and he was never one to argue with. Plus, I was not about to pass up another opportunity to be in the rainforest, especially one as exotic as Madagascar's.

The fourth largest island in the world, about the size of the state of Texas, Madagascar is a place of astonishing biodiversity. The island drifted into the Indian Ocean over 150 million years ago, and was completely isolated from the other continents. The plants and animals that evolved on this island, such as the lemur, are found nowhere else on the planet. A lemur-like primate ancestor arrived on the island around 60 million years ago and developed into thirty-two living species and sixteen extinct ones. Many other animal groups such as felids (cats, tigers, lions), canids (dogs, foxes), ungulates (deer, cattle, horses), and poisonous snakes neither arrived nor evolved.

In the last few centuries, although hundreds of new species had been discovered in Madagascar, many more had become extinct through deforestation and other human activity. I knew that the extinction of the greater bamboo lemur, one of our primate cousins, would be a huge loss to science and to the world. If we found it alive, the lemur could tell us the secrets of our ancestors' lifestyle. Madagascar is like a window into ancient times, since many species from Africa and Asia that died out during the Eocene Era (56–33 million years ago) still have close relatives alive today on the island.

Elwyn's offer, however, required serious thought. I was responsible not only for myself but Amanda. My career remained very new and unproven. I had just finished my thesis and was the most junior professor at Duke. Because I'd started graduate school later in life, the three papers I had published were paltry in comparison to the number produced by colleagues of the same age. Primatology is a competitive field, with few academic spots available. Unless I made new discoveries and wrote papers about them, my position at Duke would be in jeopardy. Furthermore, as much as I enjoyed studying tarsiers, I had not yet found an animal that had inspired me as much as *Aotus*, nor a place that had resonated with me as much as the Amazon. I needed to find this lemur if it was out there.

"Of course I'll do it," I told Elwyn.

Elwyn and I located the sites where the last greater bamboo lemurs were seen alive and I planned to visit each in turn. I chose my team for the Madagascar expedition carefully. The first on the list was Patrick Daniels, whom I'd gotten to know at Cocha Cashu, the research station in Peru's Manú National Park where I'd studied owl monkeys. Few people were as tough and capable as Patrick. He had an uncanny sense of direction and sharp eyes, perhaps inherited from his Marine Corps father. When I called him in Seattle, Patrick said he could drive on bad roads and gruffly confessed that he was fluent in French, one of Madagascar's official languages. He mumbled something about it being time to break up with his latest girlfriend and agreed to join me.

I also invited two Duke University graduate students, Deborah Overdorff from Florida and Dave Meyers from New Jersey. Deborah was pale with short, light-brown hair and delicate features, but her jaw line suggested strong determination. Unfortunately, she didn't speak French and had never been camping. Dave was tall and nonchalant, with a dry sense of humor, a tangle of curly brown hair, and a charming smile. He spoke French and, most importantly, played the guitar. As I'd discovered in my years abroad, music was a universal language and could be a key diplomatic tool in any country.

With anticipation rising in me each day, I purchased backpacks, yellow "write in the rain" field notebooks, rubber boots with deep grids on the soles, binoculars, a green Eureka four-man tent, and duct tape, which I knew from past experience had a million and one uses in the field. I was less eager to leave my daughter. Ever since her father and I had gotten divorced when she was four, Amanda and I had become very close. At the age of seven, she had accompanied me on my year of field research in the Amazon. At the age of thirteen her love of horses was still strong. She could spend the summer as usual with her grandparents and their horses in upstate New York.

In the past, I'd had a problem finding temporary homes for my pet owl monkeys, whom I'd acquired many years before the idea of studying them in the wild ever occurred to me. Now, though, Herbie, Kendra, and their offspring lived quite comfortably at the Duke Primate Center, with plenty of undergraduate students willing to take care of them.

In May 1986, my team set off for Madagascar. The airplane journey took us halfway around the world—from Durham, North Carolina, to New York, Paris, and Djibouti, the capital of the small African country of the same name, bordered by the Red Sea to the East and Ethiopia to the West. There was a long delay, and I gazed out the airport window at desert dunes, white-robed Bedouins, and ambling camels that, in my jet-lagged state, seemed to appear out of a dream. After thirty-six hours, we reached Nairobi, Kenya, where guards in army camouflage and machine guns patroled the airport.

After a further two-hour delay, we embarked on our last

flight. Rising from the great continent of Africa, our plane flew over the then snow-capped Mount Kilimanjaro and out to sea. The soothing blue of the Mozambique Channel spread below us and I drifted off to sleep. I opened my eyes to the pilot's announcement that we were approaching Madagascar. I peered out the window and gasped to see what looked like vast arteries in the land bleeding red into the ocean. Later, I found out that without trees to anchor it, the red clay soil washed into the rivers whenever it rained. As we flew inland, the land itself looked pockmarked, as if it had been bombed; in reality, these were erosion pits.

Following the plane's arrival in Antananarivo, Madagascar's land-locked capital, the bureaucracy began. Not knowing how to read French well, I filled in customs forms as best I could. After being carried piece by piece from the belly of the plane, our bags were opened and every item inspected, even the duct tape. As the customs official opened the fourth bag, he indicated that he would like something from it as a present, but I pretended not to understand. Eventually, we were released from the airport, Dave and Deborah looking like zombies and Patrick muttering under his breath.

The city that appeared before us seemed to be from a different century. Brightly painted oxcarts pulled by long-horned cattle shared the road with a few Peugeots and Citroens from the 1970s. Walking barefoot among them were the Malagasy, the native people of Madagascar, who are descended from Asians and Africans who crossed the seas and stayed. Geneticists have tracked down the Asian component to a tribe in Borneo, and this origin has been corroborated by the similarities of Malagasy and the Malay language groups. The African humans came by boat much later, perhaps 500 years ago, and settled on the coasts. The Malagasy people were united under a single king in the 1700s, who built his castle into the stone hilltop fortress above the capital.

In the nineteenth century, Madagascar was ruled by three queens. The first, Queen Ranavalona I (r. 1828–61), fell in love with a shipwrecked young Frenchman, Jean Laborde, who brought with him an encyclopedia of all the inventions known in Europe at that time, including gunpowder, and established the city's first zoo. Eventually, they quarreled and the queen banished Laborde from the island. Queen Ranavalona II (r. 1868–83) declared the country Christian. Upon her death Ranavalona III took the throne. It was not until 1895 that France colonized Madagascar and exiled the queen to Algiers, where she died. Madagascar achieved independence in 1960, but the French maintained a tight economic grip.

In 1975, the president, Richard Ratsimandrava, was assassinated six days after taking office. His eventual successor was Didier Ratsiraka, a powerful orator, keen political strategist, and idealistic leader. Eager to shed ties to the former colonial power, Ratsiraka set up a socialist government and dramatically deported all Westerners. He turned to China, the Soviet Union, and North Korea for help in building the country's infrastructure. With few exports and fewer incentives for people to make money, Madagascar's economy plummeted to become the third poorest in the world. Ratsiraka was particularly suspicious of the United States and refused all diplomatic relations. However, he believed that academics were not politically inclined, which was why in the 1980s we were allowed into Madagascar. For the most part, every international researcher tried to stay out of the island's politics to ensure we could return.

My group and I made our way by taxi into Antananarivo (which means "the city of a thousand men," and is often referred to as "Tana"). Everywhere we looked, we were confronted by a vision of paradise lost. From the stone palace at the summit, crumbling balconied brick buildings descended the hill to the Avenue of Independence in the center of town. The building housing the Ministry of Finance still bore bullet holes from the revolution more than ten years before. Crowds of beggars in rags surrounded us, smiling and asking to carry our bags. We met Bob Dewar at the airport and accompanied him to the Hotel Lido, an old French establishment now owned by Lutheran missionaries where Bob, Elwyn, and the other scientists stayed.

On our third day in Tana we were joined by Bedo, the fifteen-year-old son of a forestry agent in Périnet, located in the east of Madagascar. Bedo had been recommended to our party because of his experience studying indri, a species of lemur. Many Malagasy did not know French once you left the capital and for this mission I needed someone to translate as we traveled through the countryside. Bedo was a competent guide, and would be a good pair of eyes in the forest.

After a week of visits to the University of Madagascar and the Ministry of Water and Forests in order to obtain our research permits my team and I set off on the road to Vondrozo, five hundred miles south of Antananarivo. Vondrozo was one of the four locations where *Hapalemur simus* had been seen or captured in the last fifty years.

Our mode of transportation was the "Dinosaur," a retired white Land Rover that had been shipped from Elwyn's field project in Egypt, since at the time there were few cars in Madagascar. The national road we traveled on had been paved under French rule but had been neglected for the last two decades, and had more potholes than pavement. As we bounced along, we saw people walking along the road, two-story homes constructed of mud or bricks, and rice paddies. The remaining landscape was a patchwork quilt of tan-and-black burned areas interspersed with grassland where the rainforest used to stand.

On the fifth day of our journey, we turned off the highway at Farafangana onto an unpaved road that was a river of red clay. The Dinosaur swerved left. Patrick, who was driving, pulled the steering wheel right, but the car had a mind of its own. The left rear wheel projected a fountain of red. The engine droned louder as the tires spun deeper. I braced for the tumble. The Dinosaur stopped, leaning far to the left. We were stuck in the mud.

"Damn!" Dave unlatched the door and jumped down. The clay was as slippery as ice and he tumbled onto his knees. Agile as a cat, Bedo leaped over him. Deborah, white as a sheet, stumbled out of the car.

Patrick stood in front of the mud-splattered vehicle, scowling. "The chassis is wedged in the middle. We have to dig the car out."

"With what, our hands?" Dave asked.

I realized that we hadn't packed a shovel or even a machete.

In spite of all that training in the Amazon, I'd still forgotten some essentials.

To the east was movement. Cows? Walking Malagasy? Coming toward us were three barefoot boys and a man who wore plastic sandals, a faded gray blanket tossed over his left shoulder, and a black felt hat like he was a 1930s Chicago gangster. One boy carried a basket slung through a pole. No, not a pole, but an *angady*, a narrow shovel.

Bedo addressed the man with his right hand extended and his left hand embracing his right elbow, a sign of respect. It turned out the man was Monsieur le Président, or mayor, of Vondrozo, and his sons would help dig us out. In return, he and the boys piled into the Dinosaur with us and we took them the rest of the way to Vondrozo.

Set against a backdrop of forested mountains, the village of Vondrozo appeared as a hundred tin-roofed houses clustered in a valley. As we ascended above them on a street lined with red-flowered Madagascar Flamboyant trees, barefoot children ran behind our vehicle, calling "*vasaha, vasaha, vasaha*," or "foreigner," confirming that we were the first white faces they had possibly ever seen.

Monsieur le Président lived on top of a hill in a large, pink house roofed with orange tile and with a wrap-around veran-dah, a relic of colonial times. We sat in the living room in huge red velvet chairs opposite the president and his family, which consisted of nine children ranging in age from a toddler to a twelve-year-old boy. The president's wife graciously poured Fanta (orange soda) for us. It was a luxury, even for the presi-dent's family.

I began speaking in halting French. "We have come from a country very far away. The United States of America. Do you know about this place?"

"Yes, I have heard of your country," the president said. "I have heard that your country has sent a man to the moon. Is that true?"

I nodded. "This happened in 1969, almost seventeen years ago. The man's name was Neil Armstrong."

The president spoke to his children in Malagasy, and their eyes expanded in wonder.

I tried to steer the conversation back to our mission, but the limitations of my French made me sound like a third-grader. "We have come here because it is special. Not like the moon with only dust and rocks. Special with plants and animals."

I reached into my bag and took out a book. It was in French and filled with color photos of bright blue chameleons, green geckos, and tomato frogs as red as Campbell's soup. As the children gathered around to look, I turned to a page of bright-eyed lemurs and pointed to each one.

"There are more than thirty different kinds of lemur. But we have come to Vondrozo to find one special lemur that is not in the book. A gray lemur with white ear tufts that eats bamboo. Have you seen it?"

The president spoke slowly, with authority. "No, I do not know that lemur. I have not walked in the forest. It's better to stay here in the village." His eyes gazed intently into mine. "It is very dangerous."

"Why?" I asked.

"There is a spirit animal in the forest. Local people have a *fady* against hunting or even walking there."

I looked at Bedo, who whispered, "*Fady* means 'taboo'." I wondered what the president meant, since the word "lemur" comes from the Latin word *lemures*, meaning "spirits." Maybe there were lemurs in the forest after all?

"Since we are not local people, we will be safe," I said. I offered the book with the pictures of Madagascan flora and fauna to the president. "Please take this book as our thanks."

He still looked doubtful, but he accepted our gift.

After visiting the local Department of Water and Forests, or local park service, to show our permits, we bought supplies for our hike and hired three men to help carry them. The sun was hot by this time, since there was no forest cover. In the two thousand years that they had been on the island, humans had destroyed nearly ninety percent of its forests. Our group filed one by one along a narrow trail through the grassland. Up and down over rolling hills we trudged for four hours. By the afternoon, we reached the foot of the mountains and entered the forest. There was no more trail, and the climb was steep. Vines like giant spider webs threatened to entangle us. Half an hour later we reached the summit. To the east, across a barren wasteland, was a direct view of the Indian Ocean.

Back in the rainforest, as we forded a stream, one of our local guides lifted a rock onto the bank and cracked it with his machete. The rock broke in half, revealing a kaleidoscope of purple—an amethyst. He cracked another rock, this one glistening pink—a rosy quartz. This forest wasn't only a haven for biodiversity, but gemstones as well.

The sun dropped below the treetops, and we heard what sounded like singing. Were these singing spirits? If so, they were spirits that also smoked, as the smell of fire drifted through the foliage. They turned out to be a group of miners who suggested we camp there and sleep near the fire.

"No problem for us, we have warm sleeping bags," I explained to Bedo.

"The cold is not the problem. They say the *vasahas* must sleep near the fire to be safe."

"From what, lemurs?" Dave laughed like a biologist scorning native superstition.

We pitched our tents far from the fire but we shared our rice with the miners, in a meal that ended with homemade rum called *toaka gasy* and Malagasy conversation. One elderly man began telling a story that Bedo translated for us.

"My father was a hunter and a farmer in Bezavona, a village south from here. Sometimes he brought home forest birds to eat, a green pigeon or a blue coua. This time I went with him. I was twelve years old. It was in 1947, before the French drove us out of the forest. My father had already killed one bird and I remember I was carrying it. It was getting dark, and we started to go home. Suddenly, I heard a big splash and I turned around and looked. There was the Rano-omby-be! It was big and dark as a bull, coming out of the stream, roaring and angry."

"What's a Rano-omby-be?" I asked.

"The words mean 'big water cow,' and I don't know that is what he saw," Bedo said.

The man continued with the story. "I ran to the left and the beast chased my father, who climbed into a tree. I remember its giant head, ramming the tree trunk. My father was strong, but I could see he was terrified and losing his grip. His chest was heaving, his face pale. Only a few seconds later, my father fell from the tree, and the Rano-omby-be charged him and trampled him. Stomped him with a great fury." The old man was framed by the firelight, his voice cracking with emotion. "I ran away down the mountain and out of the forest until I reached home. The next day we found my father's body under the tree. That's why no one comes here anymore. It is *fady*."

The faces of the miners turned away from the storyteller. A man began to strum on a handmade guitar and their voices melded with the mist, singing louder and louder to scare away the Rano-omby-be.

That night I dreamed that it was years later and I had returned to Madagascar to find the Rano-omby-be, only that it turned out to be the giant extinct lemur *Megaladapis*. In my dream it was alive again, five feet long with black fur. When I tried to follow it, it splashed away through the marshes.

For weeks, my team and I searched the trail-less forest for any kind of bamboo lemur, even the one species that we knew existed, the eastern lesser bamboo lemur, or *Hapalemur gri-seus*. These gray-brown lemurs weighed only a few ounces, compared to the greater bamboo lemur, which was almost ten pounds. *Griseus* were well-documented throughout Madagascar, but I knew how elusive they could be, blending into the early morning mist like ghosts. However, we only saw three groups of brown lemurs, their tails wrapped around each other like a shawl. Not only were there no traces of bamboo lemurs, there wasn't even any bamboo.

Finally, we decided to make the five-day journey back to Tana. On the way east, we stopped for the night at the small village of Ranomafana where the French had built a hotel in 1928 because of its proximity to thermal hot springs. In fact, the name of the village of Ranomafana translates from Malagasy to "hot water" or "hot springs." And did we need a bath! After weeks of washing in cold streams, it was impossible to imagine anything better than hot water.

From the Hotel Thermal we walked across the river to what appeared to be a neglected garden with cement benches scattered among overgrown rose bushes and poinsettias. The caretaker indicated a sign and asked in French if we had a prescription. I shook my head, and he asked for the equivalent of three cents from each of us.

Reading the sign, Patrick told us, "This is the Ranomafana Health Spa. That old man asked if we had a prescription because medical patients are admitted free."

We were each led to an individual room that had wooden walls once painted turquoise and a sunken tile tub in the middle, like the Roman baths. The smell of sulfur wafted up from the water. As this was the only body of hot water we had seen in weeks other than our cooking pot over the fire, we soaked and washed ourselves well, despite the stench.

The next morning, the hotel manager recommended two men from the nearby village of Ambatolahy to be our guides,

Emile Rajierison and Loret Rasabo. Emile was slight of build and wore a jaunty red beret. His eyes sparkled when he spoke about the forest. Loret, his taller brother-in-law, had dark heavy eyes, with very long lashes. He was shy with words but large in personality. Around his neck was a big canine tooth threaded through a piece of leather. We soon learned his favorite color was purple and he had a keen ear and eye for birds.

The Hotel Thermal was set on the banks of the Namorona, a medium-sized river whose headwaters were in the mountainous highlands and flowed into the Indian Ocean to the east. Although the river remained placid by the hotel, just a half-hour drive up the road it turned into a raging torrent, near Ambatolahy. Our guides took us through Ambatolahy to the only bridge that crossed the rainforest. I stared at the two tree trunks spanning the agitated water. Planks were nailed across the two logs in *very* uneven intervals, like a stuttering H. Terror struck my heart. I prefer meeting jaguars on the rainforest path to crossing foot bridges. I placed one foot on a plank and looked down at the swirling white water. I concentrated on every step. On one step, a plank moved because it wasn't nailed down and I nearly lost my balance. Emile lent me a hand the rest of the way, laughing.

The crossing was well worth my terror, for awaiting us on the other side of the bridge was a majestic rainforest rivaling the ones I'd seen in the Amazon. Huge trees covered in green and deep-orange moss towered overhead. Orchids, vines, and birds' nest ferns surrounded us. Close to the ground I saw a shiny brown frog with eyes rimmed in yellow iridescence. A bright red kingfisher, no bigger than a sparrow, sat above the pool below a waterfall. It was a scene out of a Jurassic paradise. As I walked, an incredible peace came over me, something I hadn't felt since I'd left Manú National Park in Peru. I was back in a place where I belonged.

For all its lushness, this forest was different from the Amazon. For a start, a mile from the river, an enormous stand of bamboo stalks emerged. Seventy-five feet above me, the giant stems curved together to create a lattice-like canopy—like fan-vaulting in a cathedral ceiling. As I walked around, the light danced between the small leaves and the large shoots and formed kaleidoscopic configurations on the forest floor, moving ever so slightly with the gentle breeze to create new images. The smell of moist dirt and leaves lingered in the air like a fine Indian incense. The bamboo forest had a different feel to it than any wood I had been in—more intimate, comforting almost. I reached down and picked up one of the leaves that had fallen, or rather had been dropped and eaten, as I noticed the stem had bite marks. I saw more leaves, and as I looked closely at the evidence, a sense of hope filled my body. The search for the greater bamboo lemur might not be in vain. Something was feasting on this bamboo.

It was decided. We would camp in this forest.

At an altitude of nearly three thousand feet, the forest could be frigid, especially when the clouds formed. One cold winter morning, I waited for Deborah to emerge from her small, green tent like a butterfly from a cocoon. As we'd done for so many days before, we began our walk in the dark, Deborah a few seconds behind me, each flashlight creating a spot on the trail. When we reached the top of the ridge, we turned off our flashlights. The crisp air hurt my nostrils as I breathed, and my hair was wet from the mist. Just as sunlight began to splash into the forest, I saw movement and focused my binoculars, but it was only a black bird with white wing spots. I glanced back at Deborah and shook my head briefly. *No.*

As we continued on our walk, the stillness of the cloud forest weighed heavily. Beneath the hush, I could faintly hear the rustle of leaves and dripping water. I peered down into the steep, densely wooded valleys, then up to the tops of the moss-covered trees. My breath stopped. Another movement, not so far away. A furry, golden-red form was clinging to a stalk of bamboo, about twice the size of the *griseus* bamboo lemur. Its brown eyes stared at me; its long, dark tail began to churn; and the air filled with a growl like an engine starting up. Then, in a split second, the animal leaped away.

Deborah had heard it, too. "*Hapalemur simus?*" she asked in an awed whisper.

"It must be," I replied, thinking I must still be asleep and dreaming. Yet, I wondered, this animal was a golden red color, while the greater bamboo lemur was reported to be gray with large, white ear tuffs? Could the color indicate a mountain variety? This animal didn't seem to have ear tufts, either.

Deborah and I couldn't get back to camp fast enough. Everyone was thrilled with the prospect that we might have seen *simus*, and they were eager to replicate our findings. National Geographic and other magazines, as well as films and TV shows, have brought the wonders of the natural world to our attention with stunning footage of animals in the wild. The immediacy of these images, however, is misleading. In reality, observing animals in the wild requires an enormous amount of patience. You are required to walk trails for hours without seeing what you're looking for, or sit for days waiting for a species to show up. The burst of orange that Deborah and I had witnessed might be the last lemur we would see on this trip. Although these animals were apparently not hunted, they were still not habituated enough to be studied.

After days of searching up and down the muddy slopes and in the seemingly constant cold moisture that either drizzled or poured down upon us, our enthusiasm began to wane. Accompanying us on our treks through the forest were inchworm-sized leeches, which fell from the trees almost as consistently as the rain. They pulsed on the ground, searching for any kind of living warmth to attach to, and more often than not we ended up hosting them. They settled on the backs of our necks and clung to our legs where our pants were tucked into our boots. They buried themselves underneath our shirts, and some even whittled their way into our belly buttons. Small trickles of blood formed around each sucking point. We looked liked victims of some horror movie. To make matters worse, when the leeches feast upon your flesh they leave an anti-coagulant, which makes the bite itch worse than a mosquito bite.

After too many days of deleeching, I declared that I needed a few nights at the Hotel Thermal, and so we abandoned our tents for the hot springs. On our first night back in the hotel, we sat in the dining room where the roaring fireplace radiated heat. The maître d', Monsieur Pierre, was barefoot and wore an untucked white shirt over ankle-length patched khakis. But he set the table methodically—spoon, knife, fork, plate—and placed a fresh rose in a vase in the center of the white table-cloth. Dave reached for his guitar and began to strum the John Prine tune "Angel of the Morning."

Without warning, the door burst open to reveal a tall white man with a scruffy brown beard. He spotted me and rushed over and shook my hand ardently.

"You must be Patricia. I have been looking for you every-where. I am Bernhard Meier, from Germany. I have been stuck in Tana for weeks waiting for my equipment to be released from customs. My radio collars, my receivers, my binoculars, everything has been confiscated. Professor Rumpler didn't tell me this would happen."

As he continued to vigorously shake my hand, I tried to understand. I was sure that I had never heard of a Bernhard Meier.

"Excuse me, I must get a room and get settled," Bernhard continued. "May I sit at your table for dinner tonight? I am so happy to find you at last."

After he left, Dave strummed a chord and said, "Got a fan, I see. But who is he?"

"I don't know. But I sure know who Yves Rumpler is. He's very famous French professor from Strasbourg University who conducted chromosome studies of lemurs and found out that there are eight species of sportive lemur" (called *sportive* because of their behavior of boxing with their fists when cap-tured), "not one, as was written in the textbooks. In fact, he was on one of those earlier trips that described *Hapalemur simus* alive."

"Whoever this Bernhard is, I don't like him," Patrick said abruptly.

At dinner, over steaming vegetable soup followed by a main course of curried crayfish from the local streams, Bernhard was the only one who talked. He explained that he was a high school teacher from Bochum, Germany. He'd encountered Professor Rumpler at a meeting about primates in Strasbourg, and the Professor had asked him to come to Madagascar to study the red-bellied lemur.

"Have you studied primates before?" Patrick asked.

"Well, no, but I've spent years watching the behavior of slender lorises," said Bernhard, referring to a species of primate found in India and Sri Lanka.

"Oh, in captivity." Patrick barely bothered to mask his condescension.

Of course, I had also started out with studying primates in captivity, having raised owl monkeys in a Brooklyn apartment, but this was probably not the time to bring that up. As much as I understood where Bernhard was coming from, there was something about him that didn't sit right, especially his reaction when I mentioned that we had recently seen *Hapalemur simus*.

"Are you sure?" he asked with deep skepticism.

I explained to Bernhard that the lemur was a rich golden red with gold fur framing an almost-black face. The back, forehead, and ears were a browner gold, its ears close to the head. Because what we'd seen was much larger than the *griseus* bamboo lemur, it could only be the greater bamboo lemur.

"Why wasn't it gray with white ear tufts, like in the pictures?" Bernhard demanded.

"I don't know," I admitted. "It must be some sort of color variety. There are black-and-white ruffed lemurs here, and red ruffed lemurs up north on Masoala Peninsula, that are different varieties of the same species."

"Maybe," Bernhard said, but I could tell he didn't think so.

He left before our barefoot waiter brought in dessert, a platter of flaming bananas.

Patrick shook his head. "Who is this guy? Do you think it's a coincidence that he's here? I think there's something fishy going on."

"He means well," Deborah said. "He's just a schoolteacher."

"Yes, he's harmless," I said, or so I hoped.

After we returned to our campsite in the rainforest, both Patrick and Dave continued to theorize that Bernhard had been sent to spy on us by the French. The French had colonized Madagascar for sixty years, and they still thought they had priority on all things Malagasy. Why wouldn't they want to be the first to rediscover the greater bamboo lemur?

We were able to catch a few more glimpses of what we assumed was *Hapalemur simus* munching bamboo in the mist before we received word that Bernhard was setting up camp nearby. He had finally gotten his equipment out of customs after paying a fee, and when we went to meet him, he showed us his treasure trove. There were extra pairs of Leitz binoculars, Canon cameras, radio collars and receivers, tins of German cookies, boxes of bouillon cubes, pairs of rubber boots, and extra raincoats. There was little doubt that this man was well funded.

"I'm going to have a house built in the forest, on the next hill over," he told us. "I just can't live in a tent."

The first thing Bernhard wanted to do was to join us on one of our lemur searches, so we set out together the next day. His weeks waiting for customs had not helped his fitness, and his top-of-the-line Leitz binoculars remained unused as he struggled to keep up.

"Expensive equipment, still can't see lemurs," Patrick muttered under his breath.

The following morning at our campsite Emile and Loret arrived early as I was cooking breakfast over the fire. I greeted them cheerfully, but they stood silent with bowed heads.

Emile said almost in a whisper, "We are very sorry, but we cannot work with you anymore."

I snapped to attention, shocked at this news. "I don't understand."

"We are going to work for Bernhard. He has offered us a good salary following the bamboo lemurs for him."

The words stung, but they did confirm something. Bernhard was indeed interested in *Hapalemur simus*, and had been all along. Plus, he had dart guns and fancy binoculars. All we had to our advantage were our guides, and now he had taken them.

My face was red, and it was not from the fire. I started to speak, then caught myself. This was Madagascar, and if I raised my voice or showed in any way that I was angry, I would lose Emile and Loret's respect.

"I am so sorry," I said. "I really enjoyed working with you. If you ever want to work with us again, you will be very welcome. Please come visit us whenever you want."

I shook hands with Emile, then Loret. After they moved down the trail and out of our camp, I kicked the dirt and began to fan the fire furiously. Now there were two teams trying to find out the secrets of *Hapalemur simus*.

As it turned out, the greater bamboo lemur wasn't interested in appearing before either Bernhard's or our group. A month later, with no more sightings recorded, I received a telegram in Ranomafana. Dave Haring, a photographer from the Duke Primate Center, was coming with his Sony zoom lens camera to take a picture of the rediscovered lemur for an announcement in the newspapers. Of course, once Dave Haring arrived, the greater bamboo lemur made itself even more scarce.

A week after Dave's arrival, I found myself pacing between the tent and the fire. Darkness was closing in and Dave hadn't returned from a solo expedition. The mountains were slippery, and Dave could break a leg. He wasn't used to the lack of trails as we were. Deborah and Dave Meyers were preparing their flashlights to begin the search when a form appeared out of the dark, its curly hair frosted with mist and with glasses fogged.

"Hi," Dave Haring said. "Sorry I'm late."

"We were worried about you," I replied, relieved. "Where were you?"

"I was near the waterfall filming those black-and-green frogs. It took a bit longer than I'd planned. Then on the way back here, I saw some gray lemurs in the bamboo."

"Gray lemurs?"

"Yes, gray *Hapalemur griseus*, not the golden *simus*."

Griseus lemurs were pretty common; I'd seen about seven groups so far. But I couldn't pass up the opportunity to collect some data. "How big was the group size?"

"I counted eleven individuals. Some were normal *griseus* size, like those at the primate center, but nine of them were much bigger, the size of a housecat."

"Are you sure?" I asked. "Bamboo lemurs are monogamous. That means a male and female pair with a juvenile and a sub-adult. The maximum group size is four, or if there's an infant, five. Maybe you counted some individuals twice."

"Nope, I was close by, perhaps twenty-five to thirty feet away. They made lots of calls. They sounded different from the ones at the primate center, more like a motor. They looked different, too." Dave paused. "They had white ear tufts. Maybe it's the different kind of bamboo they eat here."

I jumped up from the fire. "White ear tufts? They couldn't be *griseus* with white ear tufts. Dave, be clear, because you could be making history here. Are you sure about the white ear tufts?" My voice was full of hope.

Dave sighed and pointed to his camera. "I was with them for two hours. I shot four rolls of film."

By "making history" I didn't mean *Hapalemur simus*, which we thought we'd rediscovered. If the greater bamboo lemur and this golden variety of bamboo lemur lived together in the same forest, they must be different species. We'd been sighting this red-gold bamboo lemur, and had been following it for short sprints, when I realized that the animal had never been studied before us. The greater gray and the reddish bamboo lemur had to be two different species.

If I'd had a bottle of champagne handy, I would have uncorked it. My mind was racing with excitement. Not only had we drawn ahead of Bernhard Meier, but we'd discovered a whole new primate species.

CHAPTER TWO

CYANIDE SECRETS

(1987)

I N THE 1700s and 1800s it was common for naturalists to discover new species. They would take out their shotguns, pull the trigger, and haul the corpse back to their respective countries to be properly examined and pronounced the first of its kind. To find a new species in 1986, however, was much rarer. Nonetheless, I would still be required by the International Code of Zoological Nomenclature, which has jurisdiction over naming species, to bring back a dead body of the animal in question. That meant a representative individual, or "voucher specimen," had to be sacrificed to science.

To describe a new species, to go down on record as being the person who discovered a new plant or animal, would be a thrill and a great honor. And to describe a new species of *primate* would be an especial distinction. But I was not going to kill a lemur to do it. Instead, I hoped that advances in genetics would enable the scientific community to approve my description of a new species by comparing the DNA in blood samples from the three kinds of bamboo lemurs—the eastern lesser bamboo lemur, the golden bamboo lemur, and the greater bamboo lemur. Of course, in order to draw the blood necessary to establish the new species, we needed to capture the animals.

The second problem we faced was finding out why these three species of bamboo lemur were living together in one forest. According to scientific experts like Ernst Mayr and G. Evelyn Hutchinson, species evolve through a long process based on ecology. Closely related species are differentiated by body size, diet, or lifestyle, usually having to do with reproduction. So what about our bamboo feeders? How could these three species live together in one forest, eating the same thing, without competition driving any of them extinct?

The third problem was the race with Bernhard Meier. After my team and I returned to the United States, Bernhard stayed on in Ranomafana for another year in his house built in the rainforest. Professor Rumpler and a team of French scientists would be arriving soon to capture the animals and conduct their own certification of the golden bamboo lemur. Our competition to be the first to announce a new species had to hit the fast track.

The good news was that National Geographic awarded a grant to me and my colleague Ken Glander from the Duke Primate Center to study niche partitioning in the Ranomafana bamboo lemurs. At the age of twenty, Ken had learned to fire a gun in the Air Force in Texas. Now a professor at Duke University, he was still a sharpshooter who could hit a monkey a hundred feet up in the trees. Ken had begun his capture career on howler monkeys, one of the most lethargic of our primate relatives. A pioneer of primate marksmanship, he'd already captured hundreds of monkeys and to have him on our team was a coup. Tall and fit, Ken sported a perfectly waxed mustache that curled upward, which made him look like an explorer straight out of a Victorian melodrama.

In May 1987, about a year after I'd first set out to find *Hapalemur simus*, Ken and I returned to Ranomafana with my old team: Dave Meyers, Deborah Overdoff, and Patrick Daniels. This time, though, we only had two weeks to capture each of the three species of bamboo lemurs and take DNA samples. As before, the lemurs were difficult to find, although we kept on coming across traces of their presence, such as little bits of bamboo they'd dropped behind as they munched their way through the forest. Sometimes, we found nibbled petioles, the part of the bamboo where the leaf met the stalk. Other times, we discovered chewed husks from the large, torpedo-like shoots that came out of the ground, or tall, woody stalks ripped into shreds. The bamboo lemurs had left their trash behind, but they themselves were nowhere to be seen.

The only person who was excited about the bamboo was Ken's old friend from graduate school who was accompanying us on this trip. Dave Seigler was a botanist from the University of Illinois and intrigued by phytochemistry. The guides called him Dave Bamboo to differentiate him from Dave Meyers, whom they called Dave Guitar. Dave Bamboo wasn't at all inclined to climb up and down the steep hills. Instead, he sat around the campfire, fiddling with little glass vials. Meanwhile, Dave Guitar, Deborah, and I collected the bits of bamboo, which Dave Bamboo would chop up, scrape into his vials, and test for proteins, carbohydrates, and poisons.

After we'd been at Ranomafana for a week, we returned to camp once again without success to find Dave Bamboo sitting by the fire with our old guide, Loret. I hadn't seen Loret since that day Emile had confessed they were going to work for Bernhard.

"Loret, it's so good to see you." I eagerly shook his hand.

Loret's grin was broad and I could tell as he shook my hand that he was glad to see me, too.

"*Manahoana? Inona no vaovao?*" How are you? What's new? he said.

"*Tsy misy.*" No news. There was a reassuring tradition in the greeting. "Would you like something to drink, Loret? Some hot chocolate?" I knew that was his favorite.

As I continued going through the motions of hospitality, my mind was racing. Why was Loret here? Why had he come back? We hadn't heard anything about Bernhard and his team for months.

After the cup of hot chocolate was drunk and the conversation about the weather wrung dry, Loret asked if he could speak to me in private. This was the Malagasy custom. It was in these private discussions that deep confidences were revealed about sick children, dead parents, desperate needs for cash, and serious disputes with spouses. Loret and I walked into the forest together for about ten minutes and then we stopped.

"I quit my job with Bernhard this morning," Loret told me, his eyes on the ground. "I cannot work with him anymore.

He is a crazy man!" I was surprised that shy Loret was speaking so much, but I could see from the tension in his face that somehow he had felt insulted by Bernhard. Loret looked up at me with earnest and pleading eyes. "I want to work with you."

"We have missed you very much, Loret. Of course we would be honored to have you back with our team." I smiled my warmest welcome. "What about Emile?"

"Emile is angry, too. But you know Emile, he will stay with Bernhard."

Things were suddenly looking better with Loret back on our team. I told him why we were trying to catch the lemurs.

Loret nodded. "We need more people. Tomorrow I will bring my friends. With them we will find the animals."

The next morning, Loret arrived with his cousin Georges Rakotonirina, his friend Pierre Talata, and Pierre's brother, Albert Telo. Once the introductions were made, I explained the plan to capture lemurs by shooting them with anesthesia darts. When the lemurs fell from the trees, our guides needed to be under them with nets so the animals wouldn't be hurt. We'd put collars on the lemurs so we could tell them apart. As I looked at the faces of our Malagasy guides, I realized this was like talking about ice cream or snow—something totally beyond their experience. But they nodded, trusting us.

Our new team divided and set out to scour the forest systematically. In mid-morning, Loret appeared back at camp to report that he'd discovered a group of four lemurs with black fur and white patches on their backs. By his description, I could tell they were *Propithecus edwardsi*, or the Milne-Edwards' sifaka. Sifakas are a kind of medium-sized lemur with long, silky hair and a sideways-jumping gait when they occasionally move on the ground. They were also endangered and had never been studied before, so this find provided a good opportunity to obtain some data about them.

Ken was already loading up the gun and Loret grabbed his bag of darts. I took the net, which was actually a hammock, and we moved quickly through the forest. Up ahead in the trees, about thirty feet high, I could see the sifakas grooming each other, unconcerned about us being directly below them. Ken raised the gun to his shoulder and fired. My heart jumped. The sifakas looked down and Loret ran with the net. A sifaka landed safely and I breathed a sigh of relief. A second shot rang out, then a third and a fourth. Ken hit each sifaka perfectly in the middle of the thigh. Within ten minutes the four sifakas were anesthetized and lying like sleeping beauties on the ground.

Back at camp, we laid the animals on a blue tarpaulin. At one end of the tarp was the equipment—calipers, needles and tubes, nylon collars, and a scale. First, Ken gently laid a stethoscope on the chest of the first sifaka, a female, to take the heartbeat.

"Sixty beats a minute," he said. I wrote this down on a datasheet.

Ken measured the sifaka from where the crown began to the base of the tail, the circumference of each bicep and thigh, and the length of the thumb and big toe. He took tooth impressions, using bellows to blow dry the teeth before applying the green impression material. In three minutes, we had an exact replica of the bottom teeth all in a row. The six bottom front teeth protruded at a sixty-degree angle in what was called a tooth comb, which was why lemurs were so fluffy and clean. They used that built-in comb to groom each other. By measuring the tooth wear, we'd be able to tell the ages of the individuals.

Ken then carefully punctured the femoral vein of the sifaka and drew blood into vials. This blood, the first taken from this species of lemur, would tell us how the animals were related as well as give us indicators of this animal's health. The vials contained a special preservative so we didn't need to keep the blood frozen or on ice, a great medical advancement, especially in the tropical forest.

The collar came next. Ken measured the circumference of the sifaka's neck and cut a blue nylon strip to the exact size. He used a small machine to clamp the ends of the collar with metal grommets like snaps. The collar needed to be loose, but not loose enough to slip over the head. I was dubious about the collars. Ken had used them on many species of monkeys, but this was the first time on a lemur. Would the sifaka try to get her collar off? Would another sifaka chew on her collar? Would she be shunned by the other sifakas?

The first sifaka was gently eased into a gunnysack and Loret attached the spring scale.

"It's 5.8 kilos," I read out. About thirteen pounds.

Finally, came the hard part. Someone had to cradle the sifaka as she came out of the anesthesia. She needed to be constantly watched and given water as she regained consciousness. Ken offered the sifaka to me, and I held her like a newborn baby. She was about the size of a month-old human, with plush black fur. As her amber eyes slowly opened, I turned so that the sun wouldn't hurt her eyes. With her pink tongue she licked water I offered her with a syringe. She was thirsty. As she became more alert, she didn't try to bite but looked around at all of us, as if she couldn't believe what she was seeing. In another half hour she was squirming and I couldn't control her powerful legs.

"We need to put her into a sack to fully recover," Ken said. "Then we'll release her and the others back where we caught them."

We took four large sacks with a sifaka in each into the forest. I peeled back the mouth of the sack holding mine. The sifaka popped her black head out and peered around. Her blue collar didn't seem to be bothering her. Then, she took one big acrobatic jump into the nearest tree, the others following her. We'd just accomplished our first successful lemur capture and release. Now if we could only find some bamboo lemurs!

Sometimes, all you need in research is momentum. About a week later, Loret and I came across two golden bamboo lemurs about fifteen feet from the ground. We both froze where we stood so as not to disturb them. Fortunately, the lemurs were unaware of us, intent instead on a bamboo shoot with a diameter of about half the size of their heads. One lemur jumped down on the ground and began to gnaw the shoot as if it were a huge piece of asparagus. She chewed through the spiny, tough covering to reach the soft, tightly packed layers and tender white inside. It took about twenty minutes before she could break the shoot off from the stalk and, carrying it in her hands, she used her strong hind legs to spring into a tree.

The other lemur, probably her son, came over to share the shoot, which was as long as they were.

My leg was falling asleep and I couldn't hold still any longer. My little movement alerted the lemurs and they dropped the last bit of shoot and disappeared. I picked up the remaining piece and smelled it—it had the aroma of fresh almonds or marzipan candy. I understood why the lemurs were so enthusiastic about the shoots. I almost wanted to taste it myself, but I took the bit back to Dave Bamboo's chemistry lab at the campsite.

Dave started to do his usual analysis. All of a sudden he exclaimed, "Holy moly, look at this!" He held up one of his glass vials. Inside I could see little strips of dark blue paper. "Do you know what this is?"

"It's bamboo," Patrick said dryly. "Your vials are always filled with chopped-up bits of bamboo."

Dave ignored Patrick and held up another vial. "Just to show you the difference, look at this strip of paper." This vial also had bamboo bits in it, but the paper was totally white. "Most of the bamboo samples don't react with the paper strips. It's only the young shoots, which are full of cyanide. They're so lethal that if you"—he pointed at Patrick—"were to eat a plate of these bamboo bits, you'd be deader than a doornail."

"But somehow the golden bamboo lemur eats these shoots every day," I added.

I had never seen another kind of lemur eating these shoots. Perhaps this was one aspect of the "niche partitioning." The greater bamboo lemur had teeth like a can opener that could rip the stalks to shreds to get to the pith inside. The eastern lesser bamboo lemur didn't have those teeth, so they ate the petioles, tiny stems of the leaves of the bamboo. The golden bamboo lemur must have developed special digestive capabilities to eat the part of the bamboo that the others couldn't. Each of the species had evolved special adaptations to eating different parts of the bamboo!

Time was up for Ken Glander, and he and Dave Bamboo returned to the United States We had captured important data on the Milne-Edwards' sifaka, but not the bamboo lemurs, although we had discovered one of their secrets. As I said goodbye to Ken and Dave, I could feel the breath of Bernhard and the French on my neck.

Not long after their departure, Loret and I were back on the trail when we heard a crack ringing through the forest. Was it a hunter? No, it was followed by a creaking and groaning, ending in a resonant crash. This was the sound of a giant tree falling. Nausea welled up in the pit of my stomach. From my experience in the Amazon, I knew very well what that sound portended. Timber exploiters had invaded this pristine rainforest. Loret and I walked further along the trail and saw a man dressed in rags cutting up a huge piece of rosewood. Hard at work, he hardly looked at us.

We heard another loud crack as a second tree began to fall. A five-hundred-year-old tree was being felled by an ax, by hand, by one man. I asked Loret how much the man was being paid, and gasped when I realized that such difficult work earned the equivalent of one dollar a day. Loret also explained to me that his uncle, who knew all the trees in the forest, was in charge of hiring men from the surrounding villages to cut down timber. As he told me this, we heard the sounds of cutting to our west.

From that day on, every morning we saw men in tattered clothes moving with their axes into the forest. Later, these same men would trudge out of the forest, each carrying a log over a foot in diameter on his shoulder. The wood would be trucked to a port and then shipped to Europe to be made into fine furniture and guitars. I was outraged that the villagers received only a dollar a day to cut down a tree that took over half a millennium to grow. I was livid that this beautiful forest that housed my lemurs was being decimated in front of me. But I didn't know what to do.

"Go to Antananarivo. Le Département d'Eaux et Forêts. The ministry in charge of forests," Loret suggested.

He was right. I had to get to the root of the problem. I needed to go to the government ministry and discuss the exploitation with its director. Even if I beat Bernhard, even if I managed to describe a new species, it wouldn't matter because the forest would be gone, and the lemurs with it.

Before I left for Tana, I met Bernhard on the trail. He too had noticed the loggers. "I cannot believe the trees are being cut down. It's like a massacre." Bernhard's voice quivered with emotion. I thought to myself that Deborah had been right when she'd observed that Bernhard meant well. I told him my plan to appeal to the director of the Department of Water and Forests.

"Thank you, Patricia, thank you for all you are doing for

our lemurs." Bernhard paused. "Actually, I have been wanting to talk to you. I want to tell you that we have obtained
blood samples from all three species of bamboo lemur. Professor Rumpler is doing the genetics in his laboratory in France
and we are writing the paper describing the new species now."

My heart sank—my worst fears were happening.

"Patricia." Bernhard's voice became intimate, as if he was
about to propose marriage. "We want to invite you to add your
information to the paper and to be an author. It will be a much
stronger paper if you include your behavior and ranging data."

I was speechless.

"We shouldn't be fighting over these lemurs, especially with
what is happening to their habitat."

I almost hugged Bernhard, thought better of it, and instead
extended my hand. "Thank you, Bernhard. Thank you for
including me on the paper."

In a paper entitled "A New Species of *Hapalemur* (Primates)
from South East Madagascar" that came out in the journal
Folia Primatologica in 1987, we named the new lemur *Hapalemur aureus*, the golden bamboo lemur. The gold from the
forest, a worthy name for this treasure.

During the long, bumpy trip to Tana I rehearsed what I was
going to say to the director of the Ministry of Water and Forests. Should I appeal to his sense of national pride? Or would
he be offended and kick me out of the country? I recalled how
it was unwise to get involved in Madagascan politics.

Once in Tana, I met up with Joel Ratsirarison, the Chief of Flora and Fauna at the Ministry of Water and Forests, who would serve as my translator. A secretary led us past a red leather door padded deep enough to swallow bullets. In the dark room, behind a gigantic wooden desk, sat a small man with sunglasses on. A huge map of Madagascar hung on the wall behind him. Like a mafia lord, he motioned for us to take a seat.

In French, Joel introduced me. "This is Dr. Patricia Wright from Duke University, who has come to Madagascar to study lemurs. She has been doing research in the forest near Ranomafana in the Province of Fianarantsoa."

Also in French, the director replied, "Dr. Wright, we are pleased that you have come to do research in our country. I have never been to the United States, but I have friends who visited there long ago." I was reminded that this country had cut diplomatic relationships with all countries except China, the Soviet Union, and North Korea. "What have you come to talk with me about today?" He looked up at me, but his eyes were obscured by the dark glasses.

"My team and I have discovered a new species of lemur," I said, through my interpreter, "the golden bamboo lemur. And we have rediscovered a species of lemur we thought was extinct, the greater bamboo lemur. This is a great honor for your country."

"That is very good news, indeed," the director allowed.

"But there is a problem." I slowly approached my agenda. "The forest where these lemurs live is being cut down for timber. This might be the only place in Madagascar where they live."

The director didn't say anything for a minute, and I began to worry. Then he spoke matter-of-factly, "The trees that are being cut down are rosewood and palissandre. Since your lemurs eat bamboo, there should be no problem."

"Yes, this is true, but as the trees fall they destroy many others. The next step is that the villagers will slash and burn the remainder of the forest."

The director nodded. "The loggers have legal timber concessions of between 750 and 17,000 acres each. They have papers to cut all precious hardwoods bigger than eight inches in diameter. There is nothing illegal going on."

"The papers were issued before we knew about the new species of lemurs. The lemurs should be the priority now or they will go extinct." I tried to sound as reasonable as possible. This man had made his career cutting down forests, and I was not very optimistic.

To my surprise, he said, "Well, I suppose we could make this forest a national park. There are only two national parks in all of Madagascar. This could be the third." My heartbeat quickened at this glimmer of hope. "But a national park is expensive. We have to walk around the perimeter, which could take many months. We have to survey and map it. But if you can raise the money, I promise that my department and I will support this project." He finally removed his glasses and looked at me. "*If* you raise the money."

At first, I was stunned, my thoughts going fast forward. I was a primatologist, not a fundraiser. This would require millions of dollars in grant money. I was a visiting assistant professor, a researcher young in my career. I was not trained to establish a national park.

But I had no choice. I said to the Director of Water and Forests, "Thank you for this opportunity. I will raise the necessary funds for this national park."

At that moment, I became a fundraiser and a conservationist.

CHAPTER THREE

AYE-AYE, SIR

(1987–88)

AS I WAS TRYING to figure out how on earth I would raise the more than five million dollars needed to create a national park in Madagascar, I was given another mission by Elwyn Simons back at Duke.

"What do you know about aye-ayes?" he asked me.

"Isn't it a large, nocturnal lemur?" I said. When I pictured it, I saw a jigsaw puzzle of a primate. Aye-ayes had front teeth that constantly grew, like those of a beaver. Huge black ears that stuck out from the side of the head like an elephant. Long, coarse hair like a possum. A bushy tail like a fox. And spindly, witch-like fingers that they use to tap on dead wood, like a woodpecker, to find grubs, in an action that is called percussive foraging.

"Aye-ayes are very rare," Elwyn told me. "There may be fewer than fifty in the wild. In 1962, Professor Jean Jacques Petter was horrified by how many aye-ayes were being killed in northeastern Madagascar. There's a superstition that if a person sees an aye-aye, they must kill it immediately or someone in his family will die. Petter saw dozens of dead ones put on fence posts to ward off other aye-ayes and their evil spirits. In order to stave off extinction, he captured nine aye-ayes and took them to Nosy Mangabe, an uninhabited island in the Bay of Antongil off the northeastern coast of Madagascar. Their descendants live there today.

"There has never been a captive aye-aye in the United States. Ever." Elwyn paused to let this sink in. "If you want funding to go back to Madagascar, I can give it to you, but you have to bring back two breeding pairs of aye-ayes to the United States"

"Aye-aye, sir," I said sardonically, and I knew I was in trouble.

The second week of December, I finished my semester's teaching at Duke University and boarded a plane for Madagascar with Patrick Daniels, who agreed to join me on the expedition. We packed four army duffels of field gear, two giant plastic dog kennels, and two Tupperware containers of mealworms for the aye-ayes to eat.

Our plans were clear. We were to drive to Mananara Nord just across from the small island on the northeastern coast, find a villager who was willing to climb trees, collect two male and two female aye-ayes from their nests, and return home in victory. Mananara Nord was the place that Petter had captured aye-ayes in 1962, and the only place they were known to exist.

The first snag occurred in Tana. The coastal road to the north was washed out from the rains, and it was impossible to drive even the toughest four-by-four vehicle to Mananara Nord—an important area for spices and the closest airport. Air Madagascar had also cancelled all flights there.

To pass the time as we waited, we visited the Hotel Colbert, an expat hangout near the bullethole-riddled Ministry of Finance building. On the front steps, we were waylaid by dirty-faced children who heartbreakingly pleaded for some *petite monnaie*. Inside the hotel bar, local women dressed in short skirts and tight tops eyed Patrick. We strode past them into the inner bar, where Frenchmen drank in the dark. One of them, Jean Luc, turned out to be a pilot.

Jean Luc's family was originally from Paris and owned a graphite mine in Périnet. He had learned to fly in France. As we explained our mission, he agreed to drop us off in Mananara Nord and return a month later to collect us and our two pairs of aye-ayes. Our return flight to the United States was January 10, and I asked him to pick us up on January 9.

Once more, we rose above the airport at Tana, this time in Jean-Luc's tiny Cessna, heading toward the northeast over landscape that had once been rainforest. The rivers were reddish-brown ribbons of silt from the clay erosion. After an hour, I looked down on a forest that was tattered at the edges, a checkerboard of slash-and-burn farming. This landscape eventually gave way to a long sandy beach that flanked the Bay of Antongil on the Indian Ocean, where humpback whales came to breed in July.

In the relentless heat, Patrick and I stood outside the thatched structure that was the airport terminal, looking for a taxi to take us into town. In the absence of any vehicles, however, we began to walk south, dragging our duffel bags and kennels behind us. The one-lane road was paved, although broken with time. We saw no cars, not even a bicycle. But we weren't alone. Women with baskets on their heads, barefoot but wrapped in bright-colored cloth, strolled languidly along the road with children following them. The women glanced at us curiously and kept walking, but the children whispered to each other, "*vasaha, vasaha, vasaha,*" and giggled. Everyone moved slowly, conserving their energy in the heat. Streets were lined with thatch-roofed houses on stilts and gleaming puddles dotted the roads. The smell of cloves from the trees wafted in the air above wooden houses set on stilts.

The city of Mananara Nord had developed as a result of the clove, cinnamon, and vanilla trades. The best vanilla in the world comes from Madagascar. Vanilla is originally from South America but was introduced to other parts of the world in the 1500s through Spanish explorers. In Madagascar, because vanilla was not a native plant, no natural pollinators such as bees had evolved. Instead, the local Malagasy were taught to hand-pollinate the plants, and vanilla pollinated by this method is said to be the highest quality in the world. Both the multinational corporations McCormick Spices and Coca-Cola used to have big operations in northeastern Madagascar; in fact, it is rumored that the secret ingredient in Classic Coke is Malagasy vanilla.

Our destination was the Hotel Roger, run by a Frenchman named Roger.

"People here do kill aye-ayes," he said after we explained our mission. "I saw about seven dead ones last week. Nobody eats them. They just leave their carcasses on fence posts." He shook his head. "I'll find guides for you in the morning. Lala knows where all the nests are. He's an expert tree climber, and the son of the man who caught the aye-ayes for Jean Jacques Petter twenty-five years ago."

"He knows the Petter story," I said to Patrick in an aside.

"This town is so slow, twenty-five-year-old news is still news," he replied.

The next day our search began. Because of the heat, we could only work from dawn to 10 A.M. and then from 4 P.M. until after dark. Within an hour, we sighted a nest sixty-five-feet above us in a fork of a tree. It was round, bigger than a beach ball, and totally enclosed, except for an entrance facing the rising sun. The aye-ayes could construct their nests made out of branches in about a week. Lala shimmied up the tree trunk and reached into the nest. He extracted his arm, shaking his head. From then on we found between eight and twelve nests a day, but all of them were empty. Had the local people killed off the aye-ayes?

In spite of our frustration, we found Mananara Nord enchanting. The smells of vanilla, black pepper, and cloves hung in the air. Many of the trees with aye-aye nests were on the edge of the beach. In the evening, the water rippled iridescent blue and pink with the reflection of the sunset. In the distance across the bay, the mountainous greens of the Masoala Peninsula shimmered.

On January 8, the day before Jean Luc was supposed to pick Patrick and me up, we came upon nest #136. Lala climbed the tree, stuck his arm in the nest, and pulled out a furry black-and-gray ball the size of a cat. The aye-aye blinked sleepily, wiggling his floppy black ears. I placed him in a kennel and he curled up to go back to sleep, only waking up when we returned to the Hotel Roger and offered him some mealworms. He stared up at us with his beady yellow eyes, each eye facing outwards and upwards as if they weren't on straight.

"He doesn't seem distressed at all," I observed.

"He looks a little beat up," Patrick replied, referring to the scars on his face. "Maybe we should name him Rocky."

The aye-aye poked at the mealworm with his skinny middle finger, which was almost twice the length of his other fingers. He scooped up the larva with his fingernail and opened his mouth, exposing large, yellowish buckteeth.

We decided to name him Mephistopheles, after the devilish way he rattled the kennel bars to demand more mealworms. He was not at all timid, and at ten pounds could make a considerable noise.

The morning of January 9 we decided to search one last time for a mate for Mephistopheles. Miraculously, Lala found a second aye-aye.

"Is it a female?" I asked as Lala handed it to Patrick.

"Nope," he said. "Look at the huge testicles. We're sure in trouble now. Two males a breeding colony do not make."

What to do? I knew the proper procedure was to return the two males to the wild and return later to search for the two couples. But I didn't want to return to Duke empty-handed, give Elwyn the thousand-dollar bill for the private plane, and say "Better luck next year."

"We'll take both of these males to Duke," I decided. "We'll capture the females another time." At noon, Jean Luc arrived in his Cessna and picked us and the two male aye-ayes up. I hoped I had made the right choice.

At Tana we obtained an official checkup for our aye-ayes from a veterinarian, received our authorization papers and CITES (Convention on International Trade in Endangered Species) permits from the Ministry of Water and Forests, and loaded the two kennels on Air France. I breathed a sigh of relief and slept for the entire twelve-hour flight to Paris.

In Paris, there was trouble. The look on the flight attendant's face was the first clue. She waved me to follow her. I saw Mephistopheles' head sticking out from the top of the kennel as he peered curiously around Charles de Gaulle airport, ears flapping attentively. With his magnificent, rodent-like incisors, Mephistopheles had gnawed a hole through the plastic.

"Sorry, Madame, just a slight problem." Calmly, I placed the palm of my hand on the top of Mephistopheles' head and pushed him gently back into the kennel. Then I grabbed my trusty duct tape and patched up the hole.

The rest of the journey went smoothly. Elwyn was very pleased at the aye-ayes' arrival until he realized how many we had brought back.

"There are only two? And the two are both males?" These were rhetorical questions. "You have to go back and get two females," he said.

"Aye-aye, sir."

Six months later I returned to Madagascar. To my surprise and joy, our luck reversed for this trip. After only a few days in Mananara Nord, Lala found two aye-ayes in a nest, a mother and her female infant. The infant was all head, about six months old, and very alert. They traveled together in one kennel on Air Madagascar.

When I reached Nairobi, I encountered a major obstacle. My ticket to JFK Airport was on British Airways, and the ticket agent told me that all animals that arrived in the United Kingdom had to be quarantined for six months.

"But we're not stopping in England, we're only passing through Heathrow for two hours," I protested.

"The rule applies even if the animals are only in transit." The ticket agent was resolute.

"But this is a special pair of animals. They're an endangered species from Madagascar en route to a conservation center in the United States Please, this is an exceptional case." I showed her the stack of papers—all the authorizations I carried.

"Oh, that's different! A wild animal? British Airways does not carry wild animals without special permission from the head of the airlines. Go check with KLM, they might allow it." Obviously, the ticket agent wanted me to disappear.

At the KLM counter I made my case. "Sir, I have two rare animals, a mother and an infant that I am bringing from Madagascar to the Duke Primate Center in North Carolina to be part of a breeding colony. I already carried two males to Duke in January, and the males are waiting for these females. I have all the proper CITES permits and a United States Fish and Wildlife permit."

"Where is your ticket?" the KLM agent asked.

"I have a British Airways ticket from here to Heathrow and then to JFK, but British Airways said there are quarantine laws in England, and I can't carry the animals."

"May I see the animals?"

I hesitantly put the kennel on the counter and lifted up the curtain across the door to reveal a quizzical face with askew, bright yellow eyes. The leathery ears turned toward the agent.

"It's an aye-aye!" The words flowed immediately from his mouth. From behind the counter the KLM agent pulled out a copy of National Geographic magazine and pointed to an article about Madagascar by the primatologist Alison Jolly. "See the photo right here? That looks like your animals."

"Yes, they're both aye-ayes."

"I agree that aye-ayes are special creatures, but. . . ." He trailed off and I waited for the ax to fall. "This is Nairobi in August, with thousands of tourists trying to get home in time for their kids to begin school. KLM doesn't have a seat available until September 15."

"I can't possibly wait until September 15!" I exclaimed. "This is a mother and baby aye-aye and they can't be kept in this small kennel for three weeks!"

"Well, it's true that we don't have a seat in economy until September," and I could hear his voice soften, "but since these are special animals. . . ." The KLM agent smiled. "This mother and baby deserve to go first class."

I couldn't believe my ears. Like the aye-ayes, I had never flown first class.

On board the plane, the flight attendant brought champagne and asked if I wanted some fruit. I took some grapes.

"What about your friends?" The flight attendant indicated the kennel on the seat next to me. I guessed word had spread among the crew about the aye-ayes. "If they're primates, they should like bananas, right?"

I decided against telling her that aye-ayes ate mealworms. "No, thank you. Aye-ayes don't eat fruit."

Minutes later, the flight attendant returned with a banana and placed it on the seat right in front of the kennel's door. "Well, just in case."

Immediately, the mother aye-aye, who'd been asleep in the back of the kennel, reached her long, bony hand out of the cage, grabbed the banana, pulled it through the bars, and ate it all, except for the peel.

The flight attendant looked triumphant. "There, I told you they liked bananas."

That was the moment that the Western world discovered that aye-ayes ate fruit! A major scientific breakthrough.

Later, the flight attendant said, "Don't you think your friends would like to come out of their cage and stretch?"

My eyebrows rose in disbelief. "Thank you for your kindness, but I'm sure your other first-class passengers wouldn't appreciate that."

I started to doze, and the flight attendant awakened me with some news. "I asked the other passengers in first class, and they all agreed that it would be fine if the aye-ayes came out for a while."

Still half-asleep, I opened the kennel door a crack. The infant pushed on the door and rolled out onto the seat.

"She's so cute. Does she have a name?" the flight attendant asked.

I looked at the baby aye-aye, her head with its giant leathery ears three times the size of her body. "Ophelia," I said. She crawled into my lap, scampered up my shoulder, and explored my left ear with her long third finger.

"What's she doing?" asked the flight attendant.

"Probing for grubs," I said before I could help myself.

As Ophelia clung to the top of my head, the flight attendant brought a glass of orange juice and offered it to her. The baby aye-aye peered into the glass and used her long finger as a kind of spoon to rapidly scoop the juice into her mouth. By this time, a crowd of first-class passengers had gathered around us. All of a sudden, a long, skinny, hairy arm reached out from the kennel and pulled Ophelia back into it. Playtime was over.

When we reached Durham, North Carolina, Elwyn picked us up at the airport, happy to see my mission accomplished properly this time. As we entered the Duke Primate Center, a loud, strange sound erupted from the other end of the facility.

"What's that?" Elwyn asked.

The noise inscreased and grew more intense—terse, harsh, staccato. It was Mephistopheles. The mother aye-aye, whom I'd named Samantha, had been silent throughout the trip, but now she let out a responding call.

"How does he know she's here?" Elwyn asked. "That's five hundred yards. Does he smell her? Is she speaking in subsound, like elephants?"

I didn't know. But Blue Devil, son of Mephistopheles and Samantha, was born on April 5, 1989, the year that Duke won the Final Four. And from the founding four aye-ayes came thirty-two infant aye-ayes, the largest breeding colony of aye-ayes in the world.

CHAPTER FOUR

IT TAKES A VILLAGE

(1988–89)

CREATING A NATIONAL PARK is not an easy task. As the minister had noted, in the 1980s, Madagascar had two. They'd been created by the French in the 1950s: Amber Mountain in the north and Isalo in the south.

First, I would have to determine the boundaries of the forest and visit the villages on its perimeter to get their approval for the park. The people in Ranomanafana belonged to an ethnic group in southeastern Madagascar called the Tanala, which means "people of the forest." As custom dictated, at each village I would need to obtain a representative to introduce me to the next village. The problem of delineating the edges of the forest would be compounded by the fact that I was relying on a map made by the French in 1960. As I had seen from the air, deforestation had wrought a great many changes to the landscape since that time. It was clear that setting up a national park in Ranomafana would take many expeditions.

The following summer, our motley crew set off. Leading

our group were Emile in his red baseball cap, Loret with his canine tooth necklace, and Loret's grandfather, who was wrapped in a blanket and carried a pole over his shoulder. Then came Philippe, the head of the local department of the Ministry of Water and Forests, wearing what looked like a blue leisure suit, and his assistant, Edmond; both wore clear plastic sandals. Bringing up the rear were Patrick Daniels and myself in our camouflage field clothes.

My typical uniform consisted of black Wellington boots, green army pants, a long-sleeved green shirt, black Leitz binoculars, a green army jacket, and a green vest. My vest bulged with essentials, including a pen, a field notebook, a small flashlight, extra batteries, eye drops, tweezers to remove thorns and leeches, toilet paper, and a chocolate bar, each item wrapped in a Ziploc bag to protect it from the rain. We transported four tents, fifty kilos of rice, and huge black kettles via porters, who also carried the packs of Loret's grandfather, Edmond, and Philippe. Since these three were *ray aman-dreny*, or elders, others carried their possessions out of respect. Accustomed to Peru and the Andes, I wondered why this island had never imported pack animals such as burros or mules. In Madagascar, people did the carrying.

I hoped Philippe would not cause trouble. As the head of the local Department of Water and Forests for nearly fifteen years, he hadn't received much of a paycheck for the last ten. There was no government funding for him to patrol the forest, so most of his days were spent in the office. His department also gave out the licenses for cutting down timber, and rumor had it that he received kickbacks from the timber exploiters. I wondered if he understood that having a national park meant that cutting down timber inside it would be prohibited, thus putting quite a dent in his income.

Just before dark we came to a large open meadow, which at another time of year would have been a swamp. Closer examination showed that this was a long-abandoned rice field. It contained nearly a hundred cattle horns arranged in pairs and stuck in the ground as if they had been planted. In 1947, the French government had ordered all the villages in the forest to move by the side of the road so they could be more easily taxed. The villagers refused, and the French government sent in armed troops, killing between 150 to 200 people. In this particular village, Edmond told us, every member had been killed. The cattle horns had been placed there as a memorial. The site was *fady*, so we could not stop there for the night.

When we were able to come to rest, we put up our tents while the porters collected firewood. Our dinner was to be corned beef, as that was the only meat for sale in Ranomafana. We were rationed to one can per day which, when mixed with tomato paste and divided among ten people, came out to be about one spoonful each. However, we had heaping platefuls of rice to go along with it, and no one complained.

At the end of the meal, Philippe pulled out a flask of *toaka gasy*, took a swig, and offered it to us. Nobody joined him except Loret's grandfather. We slipped into our tents right after the meal and I soon dozed off. I awoke the next morning to the smell of the fire burning and the sound of people talking. Over coffee, I listened to Loret as he described a sleepless night.

"Philippe is crazy. He woke me up yelling about the money in the bank. Told me not to tell anyone about it. And then he went on and on about how his life was in danger, how he was going to die." Loret was clearly upset.

I could hear voices coming from Philippe's tent. Edmond was trying to talk to him, but Philippe was ranting. Finally, Edmond joined us to report that Philippe was sick.

"Maybe he has malaria, I can't tell, but he is having delusions. Let us see if he can walk to the next village. He may have to return home."

When I went to see Philippe, I suspected he did have malaria. His face was shiny from fever, and he constantly rambled about money and death.

"My wife, take care of my wife," he pleaded. "They will kill me, but my wife and children, take care of them, please. And the money. The money is in the bank, but don't tell anyone, please."

"You are very sick." I tried to reassure him. "We'll find someone in the next village to take you home."

We walked for almost two hours before we emerged from the forest into a village of huts with walls made from flattened bamboo, and arranged around a plaza. In the middle of the space, growing from the bare dirt ground, was a hundred-foot-high pine tree, as if it anchored the village in place. As we approached the tree, a boy of about ten years caught sight of us, screamed, and ran away. Two other boys turned, saw us, and did the same. Children and their mothers scrambled for shelter, terrified of these strangers who'd arrived out of nowhere. In the silence that ensued, a man approached us.

He was wrapped in a blanket and wore a close-fitting, four-cornered raffia hat that was traditionally worn by the Tanala. Edmond greeted him in Malagasy, explaining who we were and why we had come to this village.

"The children have never seen *vasaha* before," the elder explained. "I am sorry that they ran away from you, but your white faces and height frightened them."

Later, we learned from Emile that the mothers would tell the children, "If you do not behave, the *vasaha* will come and eat you." Stories still circulated of the French soldiers who had arrived in 1947 with guns, so seeing Patrick and me must have been like a nightmare come true.

We explained to the elder that Philippe was sick and needed a guide to take him back home. The elder called his son, who led Philippe, still rambling to himself, back into the forest along a main trail. Little did we know that that was the last time we'd see Philippe alive.

We asked the elder if we could camp here for a few days, and he gave us permission. As we set up our green tents, the children came out of hiding to watch the spectacle, as if we were the circus come to town. Then, while we finishing unpacking, we heard drums and rattles and unzipped our tents to see what was going on.

Two lines of people approached us, one of men and one of women, both wearing raffia hats. The women in their bright-colored *lambdas*, or traditional skirts, sang and shook rattles made out of bamboo. The men in straw-colored vests woven of *Pandanus* leaves pounded long stalks of bamboo on the ground in unison. The leader blew a whistle, the sharp, staccato notes piercing the air with authority. This was the *ndombolo*, the welcome dance. After the first song, a woman approached us with three eggs cradled in her hands. She gave one to Edmond, one to Patrick, and one to me. We received these gifts graciously.

Following lunch, the meeting with the villagers began. Everyone assembled in the plaza under the pine tree, the women on one side and the men on the other, with the children sitting in front. I was impressed that everyone in the village seemed to be included in this discussion. The women spread mats on the ground for the elders and for us, and Edmond began to talk about our mission.

"We want to establish a national park in the forest behind your village. The forest will become sacred. That means you cannot hunt lemurs in there, and you cannot cut down the trees for *tavy*." *Tavy* meant slash-and-burn agriculture.

The elders nodded, but I wondered if they truly understood what this meant.

Then the king of the village said, "Our zebu roam in this forest. Does this mean we have to take the zebu out?"

I had thought about hunting and timber exploitation, but it had never occurred to me that the villagers would want to keep their cattle in the forest. "Why don't you put your zebus in corrals?" I suggested.

"The *dahalo* will come and steal them. The *dahalo* come from Amboimasoa in the west, they round up our zebu and take them through the passage in the forest to sell at the Amboimasoa market."

Emile explained to me that *dahalo* were bandits. Cattle rus-

tling was a big business in the west of Madagascar. The villagers kept their cattle in the forest for protection, so no one
could find them easily. Besides food, they needed the animals
for funerals and special occasions. I agreed to try to convince
the local forestry department to allow the zebu to stay in the
forest, even if the forest was a national park.

The elders mumbled amongst themselve. Then the king said,
"What about rice? We need *tavy* to grow rice."

"I see you have rice paddies along the river. Can you make
more rice paddies instead of slashing and burning the forest?"
I asked.

"Only with dams to expand the rice paddies. We could control the water with dams made out of stones and cement. Ten,
fifteen years ago we had more rice paddies, but the cyclones
destroyed our dams."

I wrote "cement dams" in my field notebook.

We asked for other suggestions. There was a flurry of conversation in Malagasy among the elders. After about twenty
minutes, the king stood up.

"We need a school here. The nearest school is eight hours'
walk away. And we need a schoolteacher."

I wrote "school" and "teacher" in my field notebook.

"We need a clinic and a nurse. We have an *ombiasa*"—a
traditional healer—"but we need more help with medicines,
setting broken bones, treating malaria."

I wrote down "health care."

"And . . ." The king hesitated. "The children need a real
soccer ball."

At that moment, a little boy brought me something the size

and shape of a soccer ball but made of intertwined vines. He kicked the "ball" and it wobbled feebly across the ground. I wrote "soccer ball" in my notebook and underlined it.

We continued on this trek through the forest, walking five more days and visiting five more villages. Every village had the same needs. It was more and more obvious to me that without cement dams, schools and teachers, health care, and soccer balls, we couldn't in good faith make a national park, unless it was for the benefit of the people as well as the lemurs.

With great resolve, we returned to Ranomafana, but bad news awaited. Philippe had never returned home. The police initiated a major manhunt. Hundreds of men, including Edmond, searched for him in the forest. After nearly a week, Philippe's body was found facedown in a stream near the small village of Andemaka, two hours from where we had said farewell to him. The back of his head had been bashed in. Had someone killed him with a rock? Or had he just fallen in his delirium? No matter how hard the police tried to determine the cause of death, there was no definitive decision.

I was asked to buy a white shroud for the body and give the widow $100 for the funeral costs, which I was glad to do, as I wanted to help Philippe's family. I attended the funeral at his home, with his wife sobbing and her brother waving the flies away from the body with a zebu tail tied to a stick. I solemnly handed the wife an envelope with the appropriate Malagasy francs inside, part of my expression of condolences.

Edmond became the next head of the local Department of Water and Forests, and he was our main collaborator for the two years during the mapping and delineation of the park boundaries. He had the courage to stand up to the timber exploiters and the charisma to work with the villagers to convince them that the park would be a good thing for them.

Back at Duke University, I faced a difficult reality. I had promised dams, schools, health care, and soccer balls to fifty-seven villages, and if I didn't come through with these things, there would be no national park. The soccer balls were the easiest to obtain. My brother Glenn, who coached a local soccer team in Pittsford, New York, arranged for the donation of fifty-seven balls. The other three promises, however, posed larger problems.

I began to write my first USAID grant. The United States Agency for International Development had not worked in Madagascar since 1972, but thanks to the United States Congress voting on funds to save tropical biodiversity, the USAID team had been convinced to start funding "green" projects in Madagascar. USAID knew that the biologists were the key to diplomatic relations in Madagascar because they weren't considered a threat to or by the Ratsiraka administration. Out of the four countries that held the most unique plants and animals in the world—Brazil, Indonesia, the Democratic Republic of Congo (then called Zaire), and Madagascar—the last was the most open to scientific research. Whenever I took my last leg of the flight from Paris to Antananarivo, most of the seats on the planes were filled with experts on fish, insects, snails, chameleons, snakes, and tropical plants.

In spite of my efforts, my USAID proposal was delayed. The letter I received indicated that the department especially could not approve the education and health component of the project because the mandate from Congress was for saving tropical biological diversity, not building schools and clinics. I was beginning to realize that unlike science grants, where the proposal is rejected with finality, the USAID staff treated the proposal like a negotiation, a conversation with both sides compromising until an agreement was made. In the meantime, I would have to find other resources until a reliable funding mechanism was found.

One day, I answered a knock on the door of my office at Duke University to find a pale, unassuming man standing in front of me.

"I'm Lon Kightlinger, graduate student in the Department of Tropical Medicine at the University of North Carolina," he said. "I heard you give a talk about your work in Madagascar last night and I would like to do my dissertation at your site. I'm studying how high parasite loads in people living in the tropics impinge on their ability to produce crops. Do you know that in Madagascar there are no data for the incidence or prevalence of human intestinal parasites?"

I sighed. "I know there are little data on *anything* in Madagascar. That's an important topic, but do you know how to speak French? You'll need to speak French if you're working directly with the people."

"No, I don't speak French," Lon said.

"Then I think it would be difficult for you to conduct a project with villagers in Ranomafana."

Lon looked up with the beginning of a smile. "I don't speak French, but I speak Malagasy. For four years I worked for the Lutheran Church in a health clinic in the far south of Madagascar."

The Lutheran Church had been in Madagascar for 150 years providing health care and education throughout the island, despite the difficult logistics and poor infrastructure. I was ready to talk business with Lon Kightlinger.

Within six months, Lon was awarded a Fulbright grant and in 1989 he began his project. Under the auspices of the Madagascar Ministry of Health, he worked with the Fianarantsoa branch to organize a team including a Malagasy medical doctor and eight nurses. Lon's wife, Myna, a nurse with a Masters in Public Health, accompanied him. Their team walked from village to village equipped with simple first aid, antibiotics, medicine for malaria, and vaccinations. In return for these services, Lon was able to test the villagers' blood, feces, and saliva for parasites. Many of the children suffered from diarrhea or malaria; Myna treated them. The Kightlingers were accompanied by Sabrina Hardenburgh, a graduate student at the University of Massachusetts, Amherst, who was studying child nutrition. Due to time constraints, Lon and his team couldn't visit all fifty-seven villages, so he chose eighteen as pilots for his mobile health care. Their work won over many people to the national park cause, and helped fulfill another one of the four promises I had made to the villagers.

But that was not the end of my challenges. I had to keep up with my research. The number of publications published and the impact of those papers were the criteria with which I would be evaluated. My colleagues worried about my future, and cautioned me that I might not get tenure if I kept concentrating on this conservation business. Not getting tenure meant that I would have to go out into the real world and find another job, possibly far from the lemurs and the country I had grown to love. But still I couldn't give up on creating a national park in Ranomafana. The rarest lemurs would go extinct if I stopped.

Since I'd encountered difficulties following bamboo lemurs in the wild, I turned my lens onto the spectacular leaping sifakas, who at up to fifteen pounds are among the largest of the lemurs. I noticed that in sifakas, as in all lemurs, females are the leaders and the decision makers. I wrote about how this was advantageous for the survival of the species. With the unpredictable cyclones and droughts in Madagascar, mothers needed to have access to the best foods in order for her and her infants to reproduce successfully.

Also predators—including hawks, boa constrictor snakes, and the mountain lion–like mongoose known as the fossa— all relied on ambush to kill. These attackers would not be deterred by larger males, and anyway larger males would require more food to survive, and food on Madagascar is often scarce. The system of female dominance and both males and females of equal size evolved for all lemur species. My papers were accepted by journals, and my hopes for tenure improved.

On my studies in the field I was accompanied again by my graduate students: Dave Meyers and Deborah Overdorff, who were studying the brown lemur and red-bellied lemur respectively; Claire Kremen from Duke University, who was looking at the effect of habitat disturbance on species of butterflies; Steve Zack from Yale University, who was mist-netting all the birds, especially vanga shrikes; and Peter Reinthal from Eastern Michigan University and Melanie Stiassny from the American Museum of Natural History in New York City, who were researching endemic species of cichlid and rainbow fish. We were also joined by the journalist David Quammen, who was working on a book titled *The Song of the Dodo*, about why the most species that go extinct live on islands.

One evening in July 1989, I returned to camp after following a month-old infant sifaka all day. A young barefoot village boy handed me a telegram on a blue piece of paper. Someone for whom English was not a first language had written on it, "God nos. Macartor Folship. Call colect 312 736 8000."

I stared at the paper, not understanding. I had applied for a grant from the John D. and Catherine T. MacArthur Foundation, but did this mean I had received it? Since I didn't want to interrupt my five-day focal sampling, I decided to wait two more days before going to Fianarantsoa and finding out what the message meant.

That Friday, I drove to Fianarantsoa in our new vehicle, a refurbished red Toyota from Japan with the steering wheel on the right (wrong) side. Our old white Dinosaur had long gone extinct. The Toyota was newer, but it still didn't make the bumpy, potholed road to Fianarantsoa any smoother. To make things worse, the right-hand side front tire blew, causing a delay.

When I arrived in Fianarantsoa, I stopped at the first available phone, in the Hotel Soafia. By this time, it was four in the afternoon and the banks were closed. I had only 30,000 Malagasy francs, or the equivalent of US $9, which would pay for three minutes to the United States on the phone (there was no way to call collect, as the telegram had suggested).

In the hotel lobby, it seemed to take forever before my call was transferred to Chicago.

"MacArthur Foundation."

"This is Patricia Wright. I'm in Madagascar and received a message from you."

"Oh, Dr. Wright, we're so glad to be able to get in touch with you. The person who wanted to get in touch with you, Ken Hope, isn't here right now, but I'll put the program officer on the line. Just hold on. . . ." I was put on hold for what seemed like a very long time.

"Hello, Dr. Wright, this is Maureen Atwell, program officer at the MacArthur Foundation. I have wonderful news. You are one of twenty-six people to be awarded a MacArthur Fellowship this year. An anonymous panel has decided that your work in Madagascar is outstanding and deserves funding. We've been trying to reach you for a while now; we've talked to your mother—" *Click.* My three minutes were over.

I had no idea how much money came with this fellowship. Maybe it would be enough to fund a few more months of research. No matter what amount, it would be helpful.

Days later, when I reached my mother by phone, her words tumbled out when she heard my voice. "Pat, did you hear the news? *The New York Times* and the *Boston Globe* have been calling me. You won the MacArthur Genius Grant! That's more than a quarter of a million dollars over five years. You

can spend the money any way you want. No strings attached."
Her voice was bubbling with pride.

In an instant, my life changed.

At first, the grant meant little things. Back home in North
Carolina, I bought a coffeemaker with a timer, and a subscrip-
tion to *The New York Times*. Then I realized that after so
many years of difficult finances, I wouldn't have to worry anymore about stretching my paycheck until the end of the month.
I could also replace my old Chevrolet, which was always having engine troubles and in need of repairs.

When I was a graduate student in New York City, and while
she was a child, Amanda had a saying for our future, when we
had enough money: "A house, a horse, monkeys, and chocolate, of course." I could now purchase the four-bedroom house
on Mossdale Avenue that I'd been eyeing, the one with pink-
and-white azaleas in the front yard and a half-acre of land in
the back. We could keep Amanda's quarter horse, Boz, whom
I'd talked about selling because his barn fees were too high.

But most of the quarter of a million dollars would be spent
on my national park project. For a while, it would make up
the funds that other donors and agencies wouldn't provide,
building schools in remote villages, supplying the mobile
health team, paying local guides to work with researchers, and
generating links between the wildlife and the people to create
a chain of trust. Although it wasn't enough money to fully
accomplish everything I wanted, at least it was a start.

Ranomafana National Park was on its way to becoming a
reality.

CHAPTER FIVE

THE BIRTH OF RANOMAFANA

(1990–91)

NOW THAT I FINALLY had some funding, I decided to take a year's sabbatical from teaching at Duke University to devote myself to creating Ranomafana National Park. It would be easy enough to request time away from my students, many of whom had expressed interest in going with me to Madagascar and helping out. But in the fall of 1990, Amanda was about to be a senior in high school and, knowing that she would be going away to college soon, I didn't want to hasten our separation.

When I told her what I wanted to do, Amanda smiled her shy smile and said, "Mom, why don't I come with you? It'll be just like the way it was in Peru." She was referring to the six months she'd spent with me in Manú National Park in Peru, when I was studying owl monkeys.

"You were only seven then," I said. "You have real schoolwork now."

Amanda smiled again. "There must be high schools in Madagascar."

After doing some research, we found "l'Ecole Clairefontaine," a French secondary school in Tana, where Amanda would be one of the few international students. Amanda was up to the challenge, so I went to Jordan High School where we lived in Durham and requested that she be allowed to spend her senior year at l'Ecole Clairefontaine. "Is that a school in France?" the principal asked. It took several meetings, but in the end the officials agreed that if Amanda took courses that were comparable to the North Carolina requirements for graduation, they would accept the credits. Amanda was coming with me to Madagascar.

Not only Amanda, but fifteen Duke college seniors who were taking my primate conservation class were paying their own way to make the trip to Madagascar with me. They instantly fell in love with Ranomafana, but the constant misty rain, and the slipping and the sliding in the red mud were discouraging after a while. Our first task was to make and map the trails inside the park. Art Clemente laid down guava sticks and rocks to mark the trails; Michael Todd drew maps; Amy Kemmerer measured the distances between the markers; and April Pulley documented the process and its surroundings with photos.

A couple of the students were less interested in being part of the team. One of them, Martin Kratt, who was there with his brother Chris, was more engaged with recording encounters with wildlife with his video camera. Martin and Chris had already made a film about the tiger salamander who lived in the streams of North Carolina. Once, I caught Martin recording a fight between an adult and baby mongoose over a piece of cheese he'd thrown them. I put a stop to it and told him that this kind of interaction was forbidden in the forest. Another time, Martin wanted to use my $3,000 night scope to film frogs mating at night. I said *no*. Martin insisted. I said *no*. He promised to fix it if anything happened. I relented. "I thought you were going to help me study lemurs," I said, but Martin had other ideas for his future. He would later become the developer of nature shows for PBS and National Geographic television.

Another Duke undergraduate, Mark Erdman, wasn't comfortable following lemurs in the rainforest. He'd been a champion swimmer at Duke, but those skills weren't of any use on the steep slopes. When Peter Reinthal and Melanie Stiassny received a biodiversity grant to try to find a new species of fish in Madagascar, I knew that Mark was their man. Immediately, Mark was put to work netting in the streams. Peter and Melanie called him Rambo. They used to joke about how someday Rambo would find a fresh-water coelacanth, a bright blue fish of ancient origins and the size of a shark. There were only four specimens of coelacanth and they'd been discovered in the deep seas off Madagascar. Finally, after weeks of trying to capture something, Rambo snagged a tiny fish with dark red fins and a yellow-orange body. It turned out that he had indeed discovered a new species of fish, which he wanted to name *Bedotia ranomafanensis*—the rainbow fish from Ranomafana. Lemurs weren't the only taxa with new species in Ranomafana.

Once the trails were mapped, the rest of us turned our attention to following the sifakas. The students especially got along well with the guides, who immediately saw the academic possibilities of being with young Americans twelve hours a day.

Emile had been to high school in Mahajanga, on the northwest coast, but had never graduated. Loret, his cousin Georges, and friends Pierre and William Rakotonirina had completed the third grade in Ranomafana before they'd had to go to work for their families.

Since the sifakas slept for two hours during midday, the guides seized the opportunity to learn English and about the outside world. They'd grown up in two-room mud huts with thatched roofs and no electricity, running water, or television, and were amazed to hear descriptions of what life was like in the United States One day, Loret asked me if it was true that by calling 919 209 1044 on the phone Domino's would arrive with a pizza. I told him that, unfortunately, the deliveryman couldn't get across the ocean quick enough.

Two groups of sifakas became accustomed enough to our presence to allow us to follow and observe them. Each group foraged together within a defined territory that didn't overlap with the other territory. Michael Todd and Georges followed Group I, which was led by two adult females identified by the color of the nylon collars—Blue and Yellow—that Ken Glander had placed two years before. A male with a red collar was equally attached to both of the females. That year, I was amazed to see after the data were tallied that Red Male had groomed each of the females the same number of minutes each day. Blue and Yellow gave birth three days apart from each other. Since females are dominant among lemurs, Red Male wasn't taking any chances about picking favorites.

Group II was much larger, with nine individuals: Red Red Male, Green Female (a grandmother with an infant), Green

Red Female (with infant), and a younger adult called Yellow Green Female. The young males born into the group were Orange, Pale Male, and a yearling. This group was large and in steep territory, and it was followed by Amy Kemmerer and Emile and Loret.

One day, I'd just returned to camp from a meeting in Rano-mafana, a fifteen-minute drive away, when I heard a loud scream. I thought someone had fallen and broken their leg. I rushed into the forest and found Amy holding an infant sifaka. Michael was right behind her, his face as ashen as if he'd seen a ghost. When I saw the diagonal slash across the baby's belly, I knew it was not going to live more than a few more minutes.

"What happened?" I asked.

In a quavering voice, Amy said, "My focal animal was Orange Male, the aggressive subadult. He left Group II, heading straight for Group I territory, so Loret and I followed him. When we entered Group I territory, I alerted Mike. Orange moved fast toward Yellow Female and grabbed her infant. He bit it and dropped it on the forest floor. I didn't know what to do. . . . Can we save it?"

I shook my head. The gash across the infant's belly was so deep that its intestines were spilling out. I went to get the first aid kit, but in a few moments the infant had stopped screaming. Amy sobbed as it died in her arms.

Infanticide by immigrating adult males was a behavior documented by Sarah Hrdy in langur monkeys from India in the 1970s. When immigrating males enter a new group and want to take over leadership, they'll kill all infants under weaning age in the group. The loss of an infant causes the female to come back into estrus within a few weeks and the immigrant male will mate with her. The advantage of this infanticide is that the male will have fathered an infant within five or six months. If the earlier infant stayed alive, it would nurse for at least two years, keeping the mother from reproducing. So for immigrating males, infanticide is an efficient system to get their genes out into the world fast. Although these were lemurs, not langurs, and sifaka females breed every other year, the same principle applied.

Later, I would explain this all to Amy, but for now I let her grieve. This was a hard lesson to learn from the wild.

In the meantime, Patrick Daniels and I had been meeting with the mayor and community leaders in Ranomafana to discuss the ongoing timber exploitation. At the end of the meeting, Bobo, a fifty-year-old leader of one of the main families in the town, asked if he could speak to me alone. Bobo owned one of the few restaurants in Ranomafana. Every time I ate at Bobo's he gave me a special dish, the hump of the zebu, which was pure fat except for the skin and bristly hair attached. Despite that, I knew this dish was a great honor reserved for respected guests, so I always ate it.

This afternoon, Bobo smiled and said that he'd heard I was encouraging different ways than timber exploitation to make money. He had listened to my complaint about the potential park entrance being far from town and how a shuttle service would be a good business. Bobo had a car, a green Citroen that he'd purchased twenty years ago, but it needed repairs. He suggested that if I gave him money to repair his car, he would run the shuttle service. I was pleased at this burst of entrepreneurial spirit. The walk from Ranomafana to the forest entrance took an hour and a half, uphill. With shuttle service, the villagers would be able to reach us easily, and if the park someday had visitors, this could be a very profitable endeavor for Bobo and his family. I agreed to pay the $100 for car repairs. Bobo and I shook hands to seal the deal, and I gave him the money the next day.

The following week in Tana I found myself having Romazava stew for lunch at the Relais Normand Restaurant with Benjamin Andriamihaja. Young Benjamin spoke English as he'd received his PhD in geochemistry at Kent State in Ohio under Professor Neil Wells. Benjamin explained to me how *lavakas* were huge erosion pits formed after deforestation destabilized the soil. His black eyes sparkled with enthusiasm for red clay, but then he turned to his real task, which was to invite me to come to dinner at the home of Professor Madame Berthe Rakotosamimanana. Madame Berthe was the queen of primate research, fossils or living, and when she became the head of International Relations for the Ministry of Higher Education all of us biologists rejoiced. Determined and wise, Madame Berthe got things done and was open to foreign ideas and research. In this xenophobic country, Madame Berthe was a breath of fresh air.

Madame Berthe had chosen Benjamin to assist her at the ministry because he was bright, discreet, totally loyal, and spoke English. The guest list for dinner included Patrick, Ben-

jamin, Steve Zack (an ornithologist from Yale), Laurie Godfrey
(the lemur paleontologist from the University of Massachusetts), Martine Randriamanantena (a paleontologist from the
University of Tana), and me. We were very privileged to be
welcomed into Madame Berthe's home.

I had a secret and I waited until the meal was over to take
Madame Berthe and Benjamin aside. I had received an official
letter from Washington, DC, that stated I'd been awarded a
USAID grant for $3.87 million to establish the infrastructure
of Ranomafana National Park. Madame Berthe had worked
hard with the World Bank and USAID to put in place the policy that made receiving money here in Madagascar possible.
In my USAID five-year grant, I'd included funding to finish
the maps of Ranomafana National Park, as well as construct a
park office, trails, bridges, and signs, and pay for biodiversity
surveys throughout this large forest. I'd also included funding
to hire a technical advisor to manage the project, an agricul-
tural expert to advise on village projects such as the cement
dams to increase production in rice paddies, and a forestry/
conservation manager. There were funds to buy a vehicle and
set up a project office in downtown Ranomafana, and one in
Tana. The grant started on August 10, 1990. The letter had
taken over a month to arrive from the States.

Madame Berthe smiled broadly at the news. Perhaps I
needed a manager for the Tana office; someone who would be
loyal and work closely with the government to get us permits?
Someone who would understand the science, the people's
needs, and the culture of both the United States and Madagascar? She glanced at Benjamin and he smiled and looked

down. I nodded and I had cemented my relationship with the Ministry. Benjamin began work the following week.

My Duke students rejoiced with me, and two of them, Paul Ferraro and Alex Dehgan, asked if they could help with the USAID project. Paul was an only child from an Italian family in New Jersey. He'd been staying back at camp with the cook, learning Malagasy. Alex was from an Iranian family that had come to the United States after the Shah was deposed in 1979. His parents were medical doctors who lived near Chicago. Both students were interested in economics and diplomacy.

Paul, Alex, and I went to Tana to find out how to access this money from USAID. CJ Russian-Bell, who was my project officer, had just arrived in Madagascar. CJ was a slim, short-haired woman around forty years of age with a sharp wit and no-nonsense air about her. She had been trained in forestry, and used the name CJ instead of Catherine to deter sexual discrimination. Right away, she explained that she was glad to be in Madagascar and she was here to help me expedite this national park project. She confided in me that *Gorillas in the Mist*, starring Sigourney Weaver as primatologist Dian Fossey, was her favorite film. We bonded immediately.

"The international community has developed a fifteen-year environmental action plan with the government of Madagascar," CJ explained. "This is the first countrywide environmental action plan in the world. The World Bank and other international donors including USAID have set up three programs: Savem; to build a network of protected areas in key sites throughout the country; Keepem, to build a sustainable national environmental governmental policy; and Tradem, to trade biodiversity to maintain funding into the future."

"Trade biodiversity?" I asked. "Most of the species are highly endangered—they can't be bought and sold."

"Some naturalists have convinced the Americans that they can breed the frogs and chameleons that are so popular in the European pet trade and sell them to gain funds to support the park system."

I frowned, but knew that CJ didn't make policy decisions.

CJ continued, "The Savem component has awarded five-year grants to Duke University in Ranomafana, Yale University/Washington University in Beza Mahafaly in the west, the Missouri Botanical Garden on Masoala Peninsula in the northeast, and the World Wildlife Fund in two sites, one in the north near Antsiranana and the south near Fort Dauphin. Each grant awards the same amount of money to build infrastructure for a total of five new national parks."

I now brought up the elements that had become as important to me as establishing the national park. "In addition to infrastructure, can the funding be used for health clinics and constructing schools?"

CJ looked regretful, and I knew the answer would be the same as what I heard from other funding agencies. "I'm sorry, but that isn't possible with the USAID grant."

After every meeting with CJ, Paul, Alex and I would retreat to our small, dimly lit office on the outskirts of Tana to work on the document on one of the first laptop computers in Madagascar. We originally had two laptops, but the first week Patrick had left Laptop One plugged into a wall socket, a huge storm passed through, and a power surge had killed it. But Laptop Two survived, and Paul and Alex toiled on it day and night to make the changes to the USAID proposal.

I've always believed that students learn the most when actively participating, and I included Paul and Alex as much as possible when I was negotiating. Networking and negotiation are key to conservation. Therefore, I brought the two students and Patrick with me when I was invited to the USAID director's house for dinner in Tana. Patrick drove our car to a gated home with broken glass on the cement fence to deter thieves. Slowly, the gates opened and we were transported out of the troubles of Madagascar into a magnificent landscaped yard edged with blooming magenta, orange, and pink bougainvillea.

The director answered the door, and we entered a large living room decorated with colorful Malagasy batiks. The director was wearing a flowered dress and heels and all the other guests wore sports jackets. We biologists were a little underdressed in our jeans and cotton long-sleeved shirts. Maids in gray and white uniforms came out with plates of hors d'oeuvres and we had to restrain our eager appetites for the cheeses and canapes. The conversation was about Madagascar. The director had worked in Africa before, and knew it wasn't going to be easy to bring modern farming methods to a country that didn't even use plows.

"Imagine! Instead of plows, small boys bring cattle into the rice paddies and beat them with sticks to churn up the mud!" She laughed.

"Maybe the Malagasy like their simple way of life," Paul suggested, bravely.

"They should have a choice," the director replied sternly. "Poverty is very hard work, and they should have the option of living a better life."

I could see in Paul's face that a "better life" might not be defined the same by all parties in this room. He started to say something, but saw my signal to remain quiet, and closed his mouth.

Once we'd rewritten the USAID document to CJ's liking, she and I signed it, and Paul, Alex, and I returned to Ranomafana. When we entered the town, the streets were filled with intoxicated people dancing to blaring music. I saw Bobo lurching toward our car.

With slurred speech he said, "I'm so sorry, Madame Patricia, so sorry. I beg your forgiveness. There was so much pressure from my family. For fifteen years we didn't have enough money for this. It's important for my family to bring back the bones of my grandfather. Now we are dancing together and I thank you."

It was only then that I realized the dancing people were holding a large white mummy aloft, passing it from shoulder to shoulder as they sang. The ceremony was called *famadihana*, the return of the dead, a Malagasy tradition. The body of Bobo's grandfather had been taken from its tomb and brought back to Ranomafana so that relatives and friends could view it. The bones were then ceremonially washed by the family elders and rewrapped in a white silk shroud. The hundreds of people dancing in the streets showed that Bobo's grandfather had been a very important person. This was the third day of celebration, and the smell of *toaka gasy* filled the air. Even children were drinking the brew. Now the body was about to be returned to the family tomb, a square cement block structure without windows, on top of the hill. We watched as the family members filed one by one up the hill, singing, led by Bobo and his grandfather's body.

The astrologer had been consulted about the timing and the location of the stars and moon in order to determine the appropriate date of the ceremony. The boundary between life and death is vague for Malagasy; the spirits of their ancestors can pass back and forth across it. During this celebration the living were conveying the latest family news to the deceased grandfather, and asking him for wise advice and blessings of wealth and happiness.

The music continued to pound in the streets; I'd never heard such a loud sound in Ranomafana before. Then it dawned on me. Bobo had purchased the loudspeakers with my money. He'd paid for a hundred relatives to eat and drink lavishly for three days. He'd used the $100 I'd given him to honor his grandfather. The ancient Citroen with its flat tires and broken engine remained in Bobo's backyard. There wasn't going to be a shuttle service up to the park. I was shocked and infuriated, but there was nothing I could do. As is the custom in the Malagasy culture, I forgave Bobo, and learned the lesson that honoring ancestors may be as important as finding new ways to generate income.

Now that the USAID grant was settled, we were able to hire staff. Mark Fenn, raised in Minnesota and trained in West Africa, took on the role of First Chief Technical Advisor for Duke University. Dennis Del Castillo from Peru was hired by the North Carolina State soil scientists to help improve production by increasing yield on rice paddies, bringing in new fruit trees and chickens, and doing alley cropping on the hills. (Alley cropping is an alternative method to slash-and-burn agriculture, where crops are interspersed with nitrogen-fixing trees to renew the soil.) Joe Peters was subcontracted by North Carolina State to provide forestry and conservation expertise. Dai Peters, his Thai wife and an anthropology graduate student, joined him while doing her dissertation on the culture of the local people.

All of the locals needed decent housing. None of the houses in Ranomafana had a gas stove, a flush toilet, a refrigerator, or electricity, which was ironic, since only two miles away from Ranomafana on the Namorona River was the Barrage de Namorona, the second-biggest hydroelectric power plant in the country. Only the Hotel Thermal had anything close to these modern conveniences. I didn't want to build new houses that would segregate our project staff from the local residents. With the USAID funds, I chose the leading five families with deep roots in Ranomafana and approached each one about reNOVAting their current houses. This tactic would ensure that the town leaders "bought in" to the project and would decrease jealousies and rivalries. When the Ranomafana Project was over, these leaders' houses, now with electricity, flush toilets, hot showers, and modern appliances, would be returned to each family.

After months of negotiations, the five families were selected, but we needed people with construction skills. Only one man in Ranomafana had experience in the building business. Jean

Baptiste Rakotonindrina was the head of the gendarmerie, or local police, and about to retire from government service. Rumor had it that he had a hand in the timber exploitation. During a long, complicated meeting, I explained to him that the park prohibited logging inside the borders. He argued that he had five children still at home and had to find a way to feed his family, now that he was retiring. By the end of the day, though, I had convinced Jean Baptiste to change his profession. He would be our main contractor and builder of the bridge across the Namorona River. He would reNOVAte the houses for the five families, and construct the Ranomafana National Park office and the Ranomafana National Park Museum.

For the time being, the staff rented a temporary office in Ranomafana so they could be close to the villages, while we researchers continued to live in the forest. We needed a better structure for research headquarters, a place to keep our equipment and books out of the rain and damp. We didn't want to construct with wood from the forest, so in Tana we purchased a prefabricated cabin made of pressed pine walls with eucalyptus floors. The pine and eucalyptus were not native to Madagascar and had been planted by the French colonial regime. The roof was constructed of clear, heavy fiberglass to let in as much light as possible. Patrick and I argued about where to erect the cabin. We both wanted a place that had already been affected by outside forces, so as not to disturb the purity of the land. I wanted to install it at the top of the hill called "Belle Vue," upon which grew non-native guava bushes. Patrick wanted a place closer to water, a site already disturbed by the timber exploiters. He won out.

We employed the aptly named Edison, the head of the hydroelectric company, to put together the cabin. Albert, the local carpenter, was hired to help. In December, I returned from a visit to Tana to see it. The cabin looked as if it had been made out of the children's toy "Lincoln Logs," but a spacious deck faced the stream. Edison had planted in front of the cabin deck two long-fronded traveler's palms and four gladioli. The scientists and students still lived in tents nestled in the woods, but we all ate together in our new cabin.

Amanda attended school in Tana, living at the Ranomafana National Park Project office, near the Tana Zoo, after school and nights. The Malagasy school calendar had long and frequent holidays, almost one each month. Every time there was a one-week holiday, Amanda would come down to Ranomafana to help follow the lemurs. She was especially invested in the Group II sifakas, describing the adults as lounging and "kicking back" in the trees at noontime while the juveniles played. Pale Male (aged 5) and his cousin Purple Yellow (aged 2) would play "tag" and "hide and seek" for hours. Then one morning, without any warning, Pale Male left the group. All the group members gave the "lost call" whistle, but Pale Male didn't answer. Purple Yellow was clearly upset and sad, having lost her playmate. When Amanda shared the news, I explained that Pale Male was old enough to start dating, and because the mating season was just a few months away, had probably found a girlfriend. We'd seen a lone female approach Group II from the south several times, lingering at the edges of the territory, but she was a bit shy of us. We called this female Judy, after one of the researchers.

I went with Amanda the next day to see the interactions of the group. Purple Yellow continued to give the lost call and sit alone in the trees. We wondered how long her depression would last and if Pale Male would come back to his birth group ever again. In the afternoon, Purple Yellow raced down the trunk of the tree and looked intently at Amanda, who was taking data. At first, Amanda thought the young female was going to bite her. But, as the sifaka bobbed her head back and forth, Amanda realized it was an invitation to play, as if she knew Amanda was also a juvenile. Amanda also bobbed her head back and forth; Purple Yellow raced away, and Amanda followed. Then Amanda would run away while Purple Yellow chased her. The game broke up when Loret arrived and Purple Yellow ran up a tree. She never tried to play with the rest of us, the adults. It seemed that as much as we were studying the lemurs, they were also studying us.

About a week later, when I was showing the trail to a young volunteer from England named Nigel Asquith, I saw Pale Male in the trees ahead of us. About ten yards from him, I saw another individual without a collar, his intended mate, Judy. When Pale Male approached Judy, she'd move away from him. He would stop, eat a leaf, and then move a little closer to her and she'd move again. We watched this "courtship" for nearly an hour when suddenly Pale Male gave an alarm call (the sifaka's alarm call literally sounds like "Sifak!"). He couldn't have been startled by us, since we'd been there for so long. I followed his gaze. To the southwest was Butch, a big, older male sifaka with a tattered ear. Pale Male looked back at Judy. Then he puffed himself up and took off at a miraculous speed after Butch. When Pale Male had nearly caught up, Butch dropped to the forest floor and ran away on the ground. Pale Male leaped back to Judy, and this time she let him come close. From that moment on, those two animals were inseparable. Group III had been born.

Back in Tana, I received a postcard from David Quammen in Borneo. He still was working on his book on evolution and was looking at forests in Indonesia. He hoped the Ranomafana National Park project was going well. His news was that he'd just been selected as a board member for the Liz Claiborne Art Ortenberg Foundation and suggested I apply for a grant. I realized this was an incredible opportunity to get funding for building seven new elementary schools in remote villages, and putting roofs on an additional seven schools damaged by cyclones.

In my grant proposal, I included salaries for a four-person health team to visit the fifty-seven villages to provide basic health care, and a three-person education team and teacher training classes. I added funding for a Ranomafana National Park Museum with cultural components. Within three months, I received an answer from Liz Claiborne. I ripped open the envelope and cheered. The grant was $495,000 over five years. At last, we had the health and education funds for the remote

villages. Finally, I had the opportunity to fulfill all my promises to the villagers. I could now combine biodiversity and
conservation research with health, education, and economic
development. Only when all these components were in place
could there be any hope for success.

Ranomafana National Park was inaugurated on May 31,
1991, a gloriously sunny day. Elders from the fifty-seven villages around the park attended. After years of negotiations,
we knew each other well now. To honor the local customs, I
had agreed to buy three big zebus to sacrifice to the ancestors.
One would be sacrificed near the entrance to the park and two
down in Ranomafana.

At dawn, the first zebu, black with a white star on his forehead, was killed. Blood flowed onto the field as the animal was
skinned and the inner organs removed for the elders' cooking pot. The rest of the meat was divided into equal piles and
given to each person present. This took about two hours, after
which would come the ceremony requesting permission from
the ancestors to establish a national park. This ceremony was
attended by all the "nobles" in the area, including our guide
Pierre. Before this day, I hadn't known that Pierre was next in
line to be king of Ambatolahy.

Albert, the carpenter from Ranomafana, had spent the
previous week carving a memorial stone for the event. He'd
selected a large piece of granite, taller than a person. Upon
it he depicted a golden bamboo lemur with a giant traveler's

palm in the background, over which was draped a chameleon with a sparkling green stone for an eye. Below them was carved the date "31/05/91." The memorial stone was erected at the park entrance before the inauguration.

Many international guests attended this ceremony: United States Ambassador Howard Walker; CJ Russian-Bell from USAID; Philemon Randriana, Director of the Department of Water and Forests from Tana, who'd suggested I set up a national park four years ago; and Edmond, who'd walked around the fifty-seven villages with us. The newly appointed Director of the Madagascar National Park Service, Raymond Rakotonindrina, was proud to attend. Our guides, including Emile and Loret, were beaming. From the United States came Professor Elwyn Simons with his young son, Verne; Dave Meyers, Deborah Overdorff, and Dave Haring from Duke University; Steve Zack from Yale University; Lon Kightlinger and his wife, Myna; even my old nemesis Bernhard Meier came. Amanda, Patrick Daniels, and the Duke students were present as well.

The ceremony began. Ten village elders and I sat cross-legged on woven *Pandanus* mats, facing the east. The sun was beginning to blaze and I adjust my white, hand-woven *lambda* and tucked my legs under me. The glazed eyes of the zebu head, encircled by bowls of meat and rice, stared back at me. The King of Ambatolahy, dressed in his traditional black, red, and brown–striped *lambda* and his four-cornered, red-and-purple woven raffia hat, stood up and called out the name of each ancestor, fifteen kings in all. Then he took a zebu horn filled with *toaka gasy* and spilled some of the homemade rum onto the ground to entice the ancestors. He drank from the horn and passed it to me. I accepted it, tipped it toward the east for respect, and downed the pungent, sweet, stinging liquid. The horn was refilled and passed to each of the elders on the mat.

Next, food was offered to the ancestors, and then the elders. As an honorary elder, I received a mound of rice served on a banana leaf and topped with the choicest parts of the zebu: the liver, heart, hump, and testes. I worried it down, knowing that if I didn't eat, I would insult the ancestors. The first ceremony was completed, and we all rose from the mats.

We took a ceremonial ride in official cars to the center square of Ranomafana. A grandstand had been erected in front of the post office, and in it sat nine cabinet ministers from the government and their entourages. The elders, international guests, and I joined them, walking solemnly to our seats. As I sat in the sun, facing the thousands of villagers, my heart swelled with happiness.

The band played "taps" as the gendarmes, in full uniform including white gloves, marched into the center of the town square, guns over their shoulders. Everyone in the crowd stood at full attention. The gendarmes fired a twenty-one-gun salute. Next, the Malagasy flag with its simple bars of red, white, and green was raised, and everyone sang the national anthem. Then the red, white, and blue flag of the United States of America was raised, and I realized (*oh dear*) that it was upside down—an easy mistake if you'd never seen the United States flag before. I glanced at Amanda and we smiled at each other.

The speeches came next, each minister and then Ambassador Walker. He said, "The United States, under the auspices of President Theodore Roosevelt, established the first national park in the world, Yellowstone National Park, as a place to preserve and protect wildlife. And now, as a representative of the United States of America, I am proud to assist in the celebration of the inauguration of the fourth national park established in Madagascar. The discovery of a lemur, the golden bamboo lemur, was the impetus to protect this national park, Ranomafana National Park. Congratulations."

This was a historic moment. Ranomafana National Park encompassed 160 square miles of rainforest, ranging from a low elevation of 1,640 feet to nearly 5,000 feet. It held twelve species of lemurs, 118 species of birds, and thousands of species of plants—that we knew about; there could very well be more. The cutting of trees would no longer be allowed in the park, nor the hunting of wildlife, although there was a special dispensation that allowed and protected the zebu that were already in the park.

I gazed out at the four thousand people in attendance, some of whom had walked days to be at this celebration. I thought about the schools that had been built, the health clinics that would be established, and the soccer balls that the children would kick around the villages.

"*Tsi misy ny ala, tsi misy ny rano, tsi misy ny vary,*" the Minister of Water and Forests preached. "No forest, no water, no rice."

I looked up and over the crowds and the flags to the green mountains beyond. Hidden in them were the lemurs, who would now, because of this national park, be protected.

CHAPTER SIX

CROCODILE CAVES

(1991)

AFTER MONTHS of preparing for the inauguration of Ranomafana National Park, I needed a break. It was also summer vacation for Amanda, who'd be starting as a freshman at Boston University in the fall. We decided to take advantage of the last summer we'd spend together, and accepted Elwyn Simons' invitation to join him and his twelve-year-old son Verne on a fossil-hunting expedition at the Crocodile Caves in the northern tip of Madagascar.

At the northernmost tip of the island, ten miles from the coast, jutted an old Jurassic limestone formation twenty-five miles long and fifty miles wide. The rock foundation, once as flat as a parking lot, had eroded over millions of years of rainfall into pinnacles so jagged and sharp that they could cut hiking shoes into ribbons. From a distance, the area looked like a mountain range of gray and crusty Swiss cheese. In some parts, the limestone karst had collapsed and formed forested canyons full of lemurs. In others, the limestone had eroded from underneath and created caves through which rivers rushed. In those waters lurked ten-foot long Nile crocodiles, which gave the caves their name. Elwyn Simons had chosen one of these caves to look for subfossil lemurs. Known as the Cave of the Barefoot Stranger, it had been named for a set of human footprints found in the mud traveling one way, inside. The labyrinth of passageways suggested that the barefoot stranger had become lost and had never found his way out.

Elwyn knew more about primate fossils than nearly anyone on earth. As a professor at Yale University, he'd become one of the youngest members of the United States Academy of Sciences after he unearthed in India *Ramapithecus*, hailed as the oldest ancestor of humans. He then discovered in the Fayum Valley near Cairo, Egypt, *Aegyptopithecus*, which at 25 million years was the oldest monkey fossil ever found. The media called it the "Dawn Monkey." Then Elwyn dug up *Afrotarsius*, a fossil that was hailed as the missing link between monkeys and lemurs.

Our team included other people renowned in their field. Professor Martine Randriamanantena, the paleontologist from the University of Antananarivo whom we'd eaten with at Madame Berthe's house, was an expert on subfossil lemurs. She'd met her husband, a famous Malagasy journalist, when they were students together in Paris, and she'd lived in Madagascar for the past ten years. Accompanying her was her student, Jeanette. Professor Laurie Godfrey, from the University of Massachusetts, Amherst, was one of the scientists who'd completed a dissertation project in Madagascar in the early 1970s and had been "expelled" by the government in 1972. She was proof that "once you drink the water" in Madagascar, you always return. Professor William Jungers, from Stony Brook University, began his research on the largest subfossil lemur, *Megaladapis*, in the 1970s. At the end of the 1980s, after President Ratsiraka allowed Westerners to return to the country, Bill and Laurie joined Elwyn in studying subfossils to find out more about Madagascar's past. As paleontologists who study the form and structure of bodies and skeletons, they were able to read the past in the bones and teeth of extinct lemurs.

Although Amanda and I had been on plenty of rainforest expeditions before, this was the first paleontology field experience for both of us. Used to the shade of the forest, we weren't accustomed to the sun beating down on us as we helped the professors and their students pitch tents in the grassy plains at the foot of the limestone mountain range. In the center of the camp was PJ, whose purple turban distinguished him as the expedition leader and who directed the setting up of the camp. PJ had met Elwyn in the 1960s, during the latter's first trip to India. PJ had keen eyes for fossils, organized expeditions with great skill, and he cooked great Sikh meals! Elwyn hired him and brought him back to Yale and then to Duke to be the head of his fossil lab and all his expeditions.

Now PJ instructed the team to build the campfire in the middle of the mini-city of tents protected with blue plastic tarps. He directed that two rectangular folding tables, also shielded by a thirty-foot-long tarp, be placed a little ways from the fire. This was the "work tent" where specimens would be brushed clean, given an identification number, catalogued, carefully wrapped in toilet paper, and then stored in sturdy boxes to be transported to the fossil collection at Duke Primate Center or to the museum in Tana.

Once camp was set up, we trudged single file across the grasslands to the foot of the monolithic limestone karst. Martine and Jeannette led, with Elwyn and Laurie following over the piercing edges of the rock. The other students and Daniel Commando, the driver, were next. Amanda, Verne, Steve Zack, and I followed the paleontologists. Bill stayed at the base with PJ to prepare for the cataloging. Even without them present, our expedition numbered more than twenty.

I kept a close eye on Amanda and Verne, as it was a treacherous trail, but they were as nimble as mountain goats. After about fifteen minutes we reached the entrance to a huge cave, whose mouth was three stories high. We turned on our headlights and descended through slippery mud into what looked like the gate to hell. Being at the end of the line, I watched the snake of lights before me descending into unknown depths.

Dark flapping wings and high-pitched squeaks exploded around us and darted through the cave entrance. Amanda winced and grabbed my arm. "Just bats," I whispered to comfort her—and, to be honest, myself. I dipped my headlamp toward my feet, and Amanda and I both jumped back. The floor was alive with thousands of quivering, translucent cockroaches. "They must eat the bats' leftovers. The cleanup crew of the caves," I joked, a little feebly. Once inside the cave, we could see the underground stream with its blue-green water. We directed our lights along the shoreline. We knew that crocodiles have eyes that glow red in the dark. Thankfully, we detected no eyeshine.

Elwyn instructed each person to take charge of a separate area about ten feet apart and start digging. Muffled echoes from our tools resonated off the limestone walls in concert with the faint trickling of water from the underground stream. The smell of wet clay mingled with the strong odor of bat dung. Twenty headlamps flickered like fireflies on a summer night as we worked.

"I found something!" Amanda called.

Jeanette came over for inspection. "Not bad," she said. "You've found a *Hapalemur simus* jaw." The teeth with its comb strongly resembled that of the living species. Amanda also found a *Hapalemur simus* eye socket, and Jeanette found a *Hapalemur simus* skull the size of a tennis ball, both estimated to be about two thousand years old.

It was impossible not to find fossils wherever you turned. As I sat on an outcropping of rock to take a breather, Elwyn came over and instructed me to move my hand to the right. He leaned down to brush the rock and showed me the skull that I'd been sitting on. Larger than the *simus* skull, it belonged to an extinct species called *Archaeolemur*.

After lunch Amanda and Verne asked if they could return to camp. I escorted them to the edge of the cave and they started back. I returned to the cave and lowered myself into a deep pit next to Steve Zack. In the luminous, reddish mud walls, I spotted a thin, gray ridge of bone. Could it be a lemur rib? I meticulously used my camel-hair brush to flick the soil away from the bone with short, directed strokes. I carefully extracted the bone, wrapped it in tissue paper as if it were a precious gift, and placed it with my other finds.

"Elwyn!" I recognized the deep voice of Ted Rose, an energetic student from Colorado. The urgency of his tone suggested he'd found something good. "Elwyn, over here," Ted called again.

"Don't move, I'm coming." Elwyn sounded as if he were far away.

The rest of us continued working, although we waited in anticipation for what Ted had called Elwyn over to see. Was it a "find"—a skull, the crown jewel of any expedition?

Elwyn finally spoke: "It's getting late, time to return to camp." He added that we should all go first and he'd follow later. Slowly, the spots of light moved toward each other in the darkness. I attempted to climb out of the pit while cradling my wrapped leg and arm bones, rib, and one tooth embedded in a jaw. After losing my grip, however, I tucked the bones into the pockets of my vest and tried again. I pushed my boots into the sides of the pit, but continued to slip.

"Here." Steve Zack appeared at the edge of the pit, hand extended. I smiled my thanks as he helped me out.

As we left the cave, I thought about the huge storm that must have increased the size of the river and caused it to rush through the cave like a tidal wave. The rising waters would have trapped the giant lemurs in a grave of clay, leaving only their bones behind. I shuddered as I imagined the helpless animals drowning in the churning waves. I was glad to leave the cave and be back in the sun.

When we returned to camp, we found Amanda and Verne sitting by the fire with PJ, one of the best fossil finders in the world. PJ was telling them how he met Elwyn when he was only a teenager, and had been his assistant when they'd discovered *Ramapithecus*. The two had been working together for thirty years now, finding fossils in India, Egypt, and Madagascar. They made an incredibly successful team.

"Where's Elwyn?" PJ asked, lifting the lid from the cooking pot. From it wafted the delicious smell of curry, onions, and garlic melting together.

Laurie Godfrey explained that Elwyn had stayed back to look at a fossil Ted Rose had found. Then I noticed the lidded aluminum pot baking in the fire. Bursting with pride, Amanda and Verne couldn't hold their secret anymore.

"It's a cake!" Amanda exclaimed. Days ago, I had told her how my grandmother had used a lidded pot, a "Dutch oven," to make cakes, and now Amanda had done the same. She lifted the lid to show me. What I saw was a little lopsided, but it was definitely a cake. Amanda was very pleased with her accomplishment, and I was, too.

"Won't my dad be surprised!" Verne said. "His first birthday cake baked in the field!"

We had to hold in our surprise for quite a while, though. Finally, Elwyn and Ted appeared in the distance, lit in the golden tones of an early sunset. Elwyn's weathered blue captain's cap sat squarely on his head, his red bandana was knotted precisely around his neck, and his khaki fisherman's vest bulged. Had he found something?

As Elwyn sat down on a camp stool by the folding table, Verne slyly moved in front of the cake to keep his father from seeing it. PJ opened a bottle of Three Horses beer and handed it to Elwyn, who took a swig and put it on the table. No one spoke as we waited for the verdict. I stood next to Amanda with my arm around her waist, and squeezed her a bit in anticipation.

"We-ee-ll?" PJ said at last, dragging the syllable into three. Only Elwyn's partner in hunting fossils for nearly thirty years could have asked.

Elwyn reached into his lower vest pocket and pulled out something a little bigger than a baseball. He opened his hands and exposed the skull flat on his palms. We crowded around it as if it were a crystal ball that would enable us to look into the past, which in some ways it was.

"Ted here rested his hand on this to steady himself while digging at the edge of the stream," Elwyn said. "He had no idea it was a skull, since most of it was buried under water. I came over to take a look and removed the skull from the mud. It isn't a *Hadropithecus*, nor is it a *Palaeopropithecus*. I've never seen a complete cranium like this before. . . ." Elwyn halted for a moment. Then he broke into a beaming smile, poker face gone. "I believe it's a new genus of primate."

A new *genus*? The implications began to skip in our heads. There were eight known extinct giant lemur genera and twelve known living genera. In 1988, Laurie Godfrey had described one leg bone that she was sure was a different genus, but there were many skeptics. Was this proof that she was correct? That would mean that there were almost as many lemur genera extinct as genera alive today. This find might require a rewriting of the textbooks.

In the midst of the excitement thoughts of the cake had

slipped my mind, but Verne had kept his eye on it and now brought it out. It had thirty-nine candles (Elwyn's perpetual age). Judging by Elwyn's face as he blew out the candles, it looked as though his wish had already been granted with this new discovery.

The following day, Ted and Daniel Commando returned to the Cave of the Barefoot Stranger and shoveled mud and clay into gunnysacks. They hauled the sacks out of the cave and placed them next to a stream, emptying the contents onto large blue tarps that had been spread on the ground. Martine, Laurie, Jeannette, Amanda, and I sorted through the mud, carefully washing any hard particle as we searched for the rest of the bones. It was a hot, sunny day and working by the stream was pleasant. At first glance, we looked like a group of village women, chatting and laughing as if we were washing our families' clothes rather than our much more ancient relatives' bones.

By dusk, we'd collected the full skeleton of the new lemur genus. It was rare enough to find an entire skeleton of anything, let alone a groundbreaking specimen. This lemur must have weighed close to forty pounds, with long front arms and short hind legs. Its curved fingers implied that the animal hung in the trees like an orangutan. The teeth suggested it ate branches, or maybe tough fruits. It had a face like an indri, one of the largest living lemurs, but was five times its size. Elwyn and Laurie decided to call this fossil *Babakotia*, the local name of the indri meaning "kind grandfather," and *radofilai* after a French spelunker.

All too soon our vacation time was over. Elwyn was remaining at the Crocodile Caves with his students and the other paleontologists, but the rest of us needed to catch a flight to Tana from Antsiranana, the closest city in the northernmost tip of Madagascar. Steve, Amanda, Verne, and I piled into the backseat of the red Toyota Land Cruiser as Daniel Commando drove and PJ rode shotgun. To get to the paved road from the campsite, we drove through a vast expanse of grassland peppered with small bushlike trees and hunks of volcanic lava that could be as deadly to tires as a landmine. Daniel wove fearlessly through the trackless landscape, dodging these rocks. He always drove too fast, which was how he had gotten his name and why we'd hired him. He could navigate perilous mountainous roads from Toamasina (Tamatave) on the east coast to Tana in the middle of the country and back in twelve hours.

I was getting worried about making our Air Madagascar flight at noon. As soon as we hit the tarmac road, however, I breathed a sigh of relief and held on as Daniel began to speed on the highway. Then came a hissing sound and a *clonkety, clonk, clonk, clonk. . . .*

A flat tire. There was no way we were going to make this plane.

Daniel Commando was out of the car in a flash, and at a

lightning-like pace unscrewed the bolts and pulled off the tire. Like a surgeon's assistant, PJ handed him the tools he needed. Before we knew it, the tire was fixed and Daniel Commando took the helm again. To our relief, traffic was light the rest of the way to Antsiranana and Daniel was able to make up the lost time. It looked like we'd make our flight after all.

We rounded the bend into the airport and screeched to the curb. I jumped out of the car to rush inside to the airline counter, but stopped in my tracks. The doors to the building were barricaded, with two weather-beaten planks nailed over them in an "X." It was only then that I noticed that the rest of the airport was empty, as if it were a ghost town.

Daniel Commando spotted a boy carrying firewood and went to ask questions.

"There's been a revolution," Daniel reported when he came back. "The airport has been closed since Monday and there are no flights out. Tana is burning and Albert Zafy has declared himself the new president. That is all the boy knows."

Daniel Commando took us into town, where we checked in at Hotel Rascasse, a seedy boardinghouse that was priced for a researcher's budget. Antsiranana, once called Diego Suarez after a Portuguese explorer who arrived in the mid-1500s, was one of the first settlements founded by Arab traders centuries ago. It was known as a pirate town, but at the moment it was better than being in Tana.

No buses were running, and all the phones were down. People huddled in twos and threes on the street, earnestly trying to figure out what was true and what was gossip. We heard that there'd been an explosion in Tana, near the Hilton Hotel. Windows were shattered and some people had been hurt. Albert Zafy had taken over the television station. Tana was barricaded, and it was apparently impossible to enter or leave. Fires were being set throughout the city. Bridges had been bombed, and it was rumored that there was no traffic on the road to Toamasina anymore. This meant no access to gas in Tana.

Someone suggested that since President Ratsiraka's daughter controled Air Madagascar, and Antsiranana was the hometown of Albert Zafy, flights to Tana might not be resumed for a long time. The only way to reach Tana by road was to go first to Mahajanga, and then head south. The road to Mahajanga was bad, the worst in Madagascar, and it could take four days to drive to Tana. And when we reached our destination, could we even enter the city?

Fortunately, the World Wildlife Fund had an office in Antsiranana and Daniel Commando took me there to use their satellite phone. Many of the roads were blocked and Daniel zigzagged as best he could. At one point, a parade brought us to a complete halt. It was a marching band of trumpets and a saxophone, an accordion and drums, playing "When the Saints Come Marching In." The crowd chanted, "Albert Zafy, Albert Zafy." A man dressed in white and sporting a broad-brimmed straw hat followed the band, waving to the people.

"That's Albert Zafy himself," Daniel whispered.

"How did he get here from Tana?" I muttered.

Albert Zafy had studied to become a surgeon at the University of Montpellier in France and returned to Madagascar to become the Minister of Public Health and Social Affairs. When

President Ratsiraka came into power in the 1970s, Zafy left to become a professor at the University of Madagascar. There, he formed the National Union for Democracy and Development, and became the president of the Committee of Active Forces, which included his and other opposition groups. Now, in July 1991, they'd declared themselves the new government. Professor Zafy fancied himself a man of the people, always wearing a straw hat and greeting the poorest in the villages. And indeed, that day in Antsiranana he strode at the head of the parade, waving his hat from one side to the other at the crowds of fans.

Finally, the parade passed and I made it to the World Wildlife Fund office. There, John Hough welcomed me in and allowed me to use the satellite phone to call Benjamin Andriamihaja, who headed our office in Tana.

"Benjamin!" I exclaimed when I heard his voice on the other end of the phone. "We're here in Antsiranana. . . . We're okay but the airport is closed. What's happening in Tana? Can you send a car?"

Benjamin affirmed that a car would arrive in Mahajanga in two days. I learned that some of what I'd heard about Tana was false and some was true: the city wasn't burning and there were no barricades, but an explosion had gone off at the Hilton Hotel, and people were marching in the streets against President Ratsiraka.

Since Daniel Commando, Verne, and PJ had to return to the Crocodile Caves to tell Elwyn the news of the coup, I was sure we'd be marooned in this town forever. But PJ once again worked his magic. He found some Sikh friends who owned a car to take us to Mahajanga. Having been to many unstable countries on his expeditions, PJ was convinced that the political turmoil would be over in a month.

"This is turning out to be an exciting vacation, Mom," Amanda said to me with irony and a touch of fear in her voice.

I hugged her. "No matter what happens," I replied, "at least the two of us are together."

In Mahajanga, we met the car Benjamin had sent and rode all night to Tana. Steve told us that he was supposed to meet one of his undergraduate students from Yale at the airport the next day. She was not just any Yale undergraduate, but the daughter of William P. Riley, the head of the United States Environmental Protection Agency. If flights were coming in to Tana, he needed to be there to meet her.

As Benjamin had told me on the phone, the entrance to Tana was not barricaded, and we easily drove down the streets to the Ranomafana National Park Project office, where Benjamin greeted us. Albert Zafy had taken over the radio and television stations and declared himself the head of the government of Madagascar. But all the phones were not down. In fact, half an hour before we arrived the United States Ambassador had placed an urgent call to me.

"Patricia, what are you doing?" Ambassador Walker said when I called him back. "I just received a message from the State Department that William Riley's daughter is arriving tonight to conduct research in Ranomafana National Park. I'm sorry, but we can't take responsibility for her, not in this political climate. We're in the middle of a revolution! You must convince her go home at once."

Steve and I met Alison Riley at the airport. She was excited to be in Madagascar, but we told her that thousands of people were marching in the streets, and there were looters downtown. Alison spent the night in a nearby hotel, and in the morning a car arrived to take the three of us to the embassy. Our meeting with the Ambassador was short. "There is a plane leaving Madagascar for Paris tomorrow night, and you all are going to be on it." His words left no room for argument, and I wasn't sure if any of us wanted to make one. Although mass demonstrations had been going on peacefully in Tana for weeks, it seemed like the tension between the protestors and the government was coming to a head. We could all be in great danger if we didn't leave Madagascar.

Back at the Ranomafana office, which was located in the southern part of Tana, we watched hundreds of protestors pass by on their way to the president's palace ten kilometers down the road. Gleaming white, the residence looked like the Taj Mahal. The interior was supposed to be opulent, and the faucets in the bathrooms were rumored to be made of gold. Many people felt this had not been the best way to spend the international aid being given to one of the poorest countries in the world.

"Down with Ratsiraka, banish corruption! Down with Ratsiraka, up with justice!" the protestors shouted.

Benjamin explained to us that Albert Zafy was supported by the Catholic, Evangelical Christian, and Lutheran churches. He was calling for a change of government to end corruption. The opposition that he was a part of alleged that President Ratsiraka had ruled for seventeen years according to decisions based on astrology and divination; in fact, his astrologer was his chief of staff.

We continued to watch as the protestors, mostly government workers and church members, marched by our office, chanting and singing hymns. Three cars at the end of the parade represented the three churches joined together in this united effort. About sixty minutes afterward, Amanda thought she heard gunshots, but I wasn't so sure. Hours later, the cars returned, draped with human bodies in the way a hunter's truck might be with the corpses of deer. I gasped, and tried to shield Amanda from the sight, but it was too late. Tears in our eyes, we saw the cars drive slowly by as if in a funeral procession, followed by crying and wailing people. The day was blazing sunshine, but the air felt heavy with blood. Later, I learned that land-mines had exploded near the president's residence, and helicopters had shot at the people from the air. Around 400,000 people had participated in the protests, and more than thirty people had been killed.

The next evening, the United States embassy car came to pick us up. At the airport, there were no long lines or customs agents or officials to look at our passports. Verne was back with Elwyn and the others at the Crocodile Caves, and we hoped they were safe, isolated in the caves. Earlier, I had contacted John Hough at the World Wildlife Fund office in Antsiranana to get word to Elwyn that we were soon to leave the country and he should get out as soon as he could. None of us knew how long this crisis would last or when we'd be able to return to Madagascar.

On August 11, 1991, Amanda, Steve, Alison, and I boarded

an Air France flight to Paris, escaping the turmoil of revolution. Two weeks later, Elwyn, PJ, Laurie, Bill, and Verne caught the last plane out of the country for six months. Those left behind weren't so lucky. In October 1991, President Ratsiraka lost almost all of his power and agreed to hold multiparty elections. It would be more than a year before those elections took place, and Albert Zafy finally became president, in March 1993. The country was determined to be safe enough for Westerners to return long before that, but I'd never forget the instability lying beneath the surface of the island's politics, so far from the peaceful rainforest.

CHAPTER SEVEN

LIGHTNING STRIKES

(1991–92)

IT WAS NOT ONLY Madagascar that was experiencing upheaval in 1991. Both my professional and personal life were going through some major changes. In the fall, I made a tough decision and left Duke to start a new job as an associate professor at Stony Brook University on Long Island. While I would miss working with Elwyn Simons and my other colleagues at the Duke Primate Center, I knew this was the right step for me to take in my career. First, the Stony Brook promotions committeee had reviewed my career and given me tenure. Secondly, Stony Brook was allowing me to spend six months in the classroom and the other six conducting research in Madagascar. It was an offer I couldn't refuse.

Amanda, about to start college at Boston University, helped me find a modern, four-bedroom house facing Long Island Sound. In the evening from the deck we could see the lights of Connecticut across the water. Our owl monkeys had moved with us and lived in the backyard in a seaside cage. At Stony Brook, I discovered a new world of friends. Charlie Janson, whom I'd known from my years researching owl monkeys, was now a professor there. His wife, Frederica, helped me establish the Institute for the Conservation of Tropical Environments to enable me to pursue the conservation aspect of my life. Another one of my close colleagues was John Fleagle, who'd taken care of my owl monkeys while I was in the Amazon.

Two days after I started teaching at Stony Brook, I saw a man walking down the hall of the Department of Anthropology with Lawrence Martin, the department head. This man was tall—well over six feet—thin, and so pale he was nearly translucent. His hair was short, sandy blond, and parted in the middle. Behind wire-rimmed, European-looking glasses, he looked a little dazed. He appeared to be just as much a newcomer as I was, so I smiled broadly and stretched out my hand to greet him.

With the charm of an ambassador, Lawrence turned to the man: "This is Pat Wright. She's a primatologist who works in Madagascar. She's only arrived here this week from Duke University. We were very lucky to entice her away from Duke."

"And Pat," Lawrence continued, "this is our Fulbright scholar who has just arrived from the University of Helsinki, Finland. Jukka Jernvall is a paleontologist—we went on excavations together in Turkey."

"I study teeth," Jukka said.

Something about Jukka instantly appealed to me, and I knew that in the coming months we'd get to know each other better.

Toward the end of the year, I had the opportunity to return to Madagascar. John Cadle, a herpetologist at the Natural

Academy of Sciences in Philadelphia, had learned that the boa constrictors of South America were closely related to those in Madagascar, which implied a connection dating back to the period when Africa and South America had been joined in a land mass called Gondwanaland. John had arrived in Ranomafana to look at the morphology of snakes. He wanted to scale Mount Maharira, the highest peak in Ranomafana National Park, and I wanted to see if lemurs lived up there. From aerial photos the summit looked bare of trees, and we wondered if it was the site of an ancient Malagasy farm.

John and I put together a team including Loret, Dave Haring to take photos, and my brother Ted, who worked in construction and wanted to spend his vacation in Madagascar. Isabel Constable, a student from Boston who was interested in studying chameleons; Loret; Richard Ramandrapihaona, a young Ranomafana boy who loved frogs and would be our cook; John; and I drove three hours along the bumpy road to Sahavondronana to ask the elders of the Betsileo, a highland ethnic group, for permission to climb the mountain.

Sahavondronana consisted of twenty rectangular huts constructed of dried mud over lashed sticks. The outside of each hut was cracked like the bottom a lake in drought and capped with a roof of bundled grass. Chimneys were unheard of, so smoke seeped through the thatching and created a charcoal veneer on the wooden window frames. Yet the village had a tidy appearance, the bare ground between the dwellings swept clean by the women each morning. The spacing of the houses reminded me of the Malagasy saying *tsy maisana ny trano* ("let not your house cast a shadow on your neighbor's house").

Tradition required that the door of each house faced west; only the ancestors had the right to enter a house from the east.

An elder motioned for us to come in through a royal-blue door. The smoke inside stung my eyes. Five elders were seated on the bed, each of whom extended his hand to us. I gripped my right elbow with my left hand in a sign of respect and bowed slightly. Rakoto, the seventy-year-old king of the village, motioned for us to sit on a wooden bench that wasn't quite wide enough to fit our backsides. More Malagasy entered the room, shook hands with us, bowed, and sat down on a handmade *Pandanus* mat on the floor.

After a silence, Rakoto began to speak and Loret translated. "We are honored to have you visit us in our humble village. You are very welcome here."

Loret introduced John as a biologist who studied snakes and me as the mother of Ranomafana and a professor who studied lemurs. The villagers knew me as we'd built a school in Sahavondronana after the inauguration of the park. Loret explained that we'd come to ask permission to climb to the summit of Mount Maharira.

Rakoto shook his head. "The mountain is haunted. The ancestors have warned not to go there."

I whispered to Loret to explain that we wanted to see the plants and animals that lived on the top of the mountain. Rakoto finally agreed that two of the elders would guide us to Mount Maharira with porters, but that they'd leave everything at the foot of the mountain and not follow us to the summit. That was enough, and we thanked the village people profusely.

One week later, our team headed through the savannah toward the southwestern boundaries of Ranomafana National Park. Rakoto himself led us, in a *lambda* thrown over his shoulders, shorts, clear plastic sandals with broken straps, and a handmade raffia hat. He was followed by another elder named Ramy, John Cadle, and myself. Dave Haring and my brother Ted were next, each carrying photo and video equipment. Richard Ramandrapihaona brought up the rear, making sure there were no stragglers. The porters, without whom we wouldn't have been able to make the trip, had gone ahead of us.

At noon, we all stopped for lunch. From my backpack, I took out a sandwich and offered it to Ramy, who opened the two halves of the baguette and sniffed the cheese inside. He took a bite, immediately spat it out onto the ground, and handed the sandwich back to me. Loret explained that this was the first time Ramy had tasted cheese, and he didn't think it was food. I handed Ramy a banana and some peanuts, which he did eat. The porters begin to talk among themselves and Loret explained that the sandwiches were not enough and that they wouldn't continue without a meal of rice. I said that we didn't have time to cook if we wanted to reach the base of the mountain by nightfall. But the porters shook their heads, so we built a fire and prepared the rice.

By dark, we were exhausted from trudging eight hours in the rain without a trail. We set up camp on high ground surrounded by swamp. The porters left us and only Rakoto and Ramy from Sahavondronana stayed. The next morning, it was drizzling and John predicted it would take us five hours to get to the top. Ramy went first with the machete, cutting our way, and the rest of us followed, carrying our extra packs. We moved slowly in the wet, slippery forest among orchids drooping from tree branches and lush, broad ferns. Dave paused to photograph tiny red mushrooms, and Ted videotaped a paradise flycatcher, a bright orange bird with blue rings around its eyes, as it sat on its nest.

As the steepness increased, the trees became rooted on boulders rather than the ground, leaving huge chasms between each moss-covered root. One slip could mean a broken foot or a twisted ankle. The surrounding mist also made it difficult to see.

Rakoto stopped. "We are here," he proclaimed. "The summit is only a few minutes away." I put down my pack exhausted, but happy that we were almost there.

"Great, let's go," John said impatiently, misinterpreting the king's hesitance. It had been difficult during this trip for John not to charge ahead and go first, but Malagasy custom decreed that a village elder must lead.

"No, we cannot go further," Rakoto said.

And then it hit.

BAROOM.

Was it a cannon? The depth and breadth of the boom almost made me jump out of my body.

Rakoto and Ramy dropped to their knees, their heads bowed, and moaned as if they were in pain. The rest of us except for John instinctively following them and kneeled as well.

"It's just thunder," John said.

"It's the ancestors," corrected Loret. "The ancestors are angry that we are here."

"What do we do?" I asked.

"The ancestors might accept an offering," Loret suggested, after consulting with Rakoto.

At first, John scoffed at the idea. Then his eyes lit up as he remembered the flask in his backpack that contained a single malt whiskey. He handed the flask to Rakoto. Still on his knees, Rakoto turned to the east and began to chant. With each ancestor's name, his voice grew louder. The birds were quiet and the air was still except for the wailing voice of the king. After ten minutes of pleading with the ancestors, he poured a capful of whiskey and threw it on the ground toward the east. John winced a little to see his expensive liquor treated in such a manner. Rakoto poured another capful and drank it quickly, then poured a third and passed it to John. All of us followed the custom, chugging our caps in turn. Finally, Rakoto announced that our offering had been accepted by the ancestors and we could climb to the summit.

John charged up the cliff and I followed quickly before the ancestors could change their minds. Keeping my eyes on my feet, I didn't look up until I reached the top. What I saw took my breath away.

"Oh my God," I said. "It's magnificent. I can see all the way to the Indian Ocean."

Laid out in a 360-degree panorama was Ranomafana National Park, mountain after mountain, covered in rainforest. The pebbly green stretched out like a carpet on every side, and I imagined all the lemurs and chameleons living inside this majestic paradise. We were more than 4,200 feet above sea level. However, the top of the granite mountain was as bald and flat as a parking lot. There were no trees, just nubbly

plants that looked like cactus and short desert plants belong-
ing to the species *Kalanchoe*. John and I had been wrong to
think there might have been an ancient farm up here, as there
wasn't any soil to grow anything. We put up our green four-
man Eureka tents. Since there was no dirt to stake them in,
they looked precarious, balancing on the bare rock.

John was eager to explore. "Listen," he said, cocking his
head toward a big gray boulder. "It's a frog."

"No, it's water dripping," I challenged.

"It's a frog," John insisted. "Come on, Richard, let's prove
Pat wrong." And the two of them disappeared into the narrow
opening in the boulder.

I drank in the view again, marveling at the sight of distant,
tree-covered mountains. Then I noticed the ominous black
clouds to the east. One second the sun was bright, and then darkness, as if someone had turned off the lights. Fortunately, John
and Richard returned just as the rain started to fall. Oblivious
to the menacing clouds, John held up something in his hands.

"It was a frog!"

John spread his palms to reveal a frog about the size of the
Hope Diamond. It had a deep chocolate-brown body beneath
a marbled pattern of Day-Glo green, like a hand-painted Eas-
ter egg. We could only admire it for a few seconds before the
storm hit.

The rain fell in pulsing sheets as we ran for cover in a place
without any. The raindrops turned to hail the size of golf
balls. Lightning pierced the sky, thunder following on its heels.
I remembered my mother's saying, "If lightning is followed
immediately by thunder, the storm is on top of you."

BAROOM. FLASH. The thunder and lighting were one.

My mother's voice reverberated in my head. "Never stand in an open place in a thunderstorm because lightning strikes the tallest object." I thought we were going to die.

We were, in fact, the tallest things on this bald mountaintop. The lightning jolted the world into brightness again, a bolt so close I thought I might touch it. The clap of the thunder reverberated through my body. I turned away from the wind and saw Rakoto crouched under a rock, shivering. A flash of lightning lit up the fear of the ancestors in his eyes. Another bolt pierced the sky like the cut from a knife.

And then, just as suddenly as it had started, the storm was over. The darkness brightened and the sun shone over the soaked landscape. Amazingly enough, no one had been struck by lightning. John even had the jewel-like frog cradled in his hands (it did turn out to be a new species, *Mantidactylus elegans*). Rakoto was shaking, but still present. Ramy, on the other hand, had fled. The tents had also not fared well; three of them had blown away. That night, we all slept in the one, salvaged tent.

We stayed only one night on the summit of Mount Maharira. The plan was to camp at the foot of the mountain for five days of biodiversity studies. The problem was that the foot of the mountain was a swamp—a great place to find frogs and snakes, but a hard place to dry our tents, much less sleep dry. We found an island with a minimum of moisture, set up camp, and built a fire for lunch. Ted took off to shoot video while Dave dried his lenses.

John began to teach Isabel, who was interested in the behavior and ecology of chameleons. Up until then no one had ever studied chameleon behavior in the wild, and she wanted to learn from John Cadle.

Ted arrived late for his lunch of cold rice and beans, animated about the red-bellied lemur family that he'd just videotaped. He showed us how the plush adults groomed each other vigorously as the juveniles and subadults play-wrestled. Then a male walked along a branch, lowered his head like a bull about to charge, and rubbed the top of his head on the branch. When he lifted his head, his fur was covered with brown goo from a scent gland, giving him a flat-top hairstyle. I realized that this was the breeding season and this fancy display was to impress a female.

Ted had captured excellent footage. The camera continued to roll and swooped down to the forest floor, where an animal came into the frame. The diminutive, gray-brown, fox-like creature sat on its haunches near a small bush about a yard from the camera. Staring into the lens, it scratched behind its left ear with its left foot and then yawned. As the camera zoomed into its narrow little mouth, I realized it had no teeth. This animal had to be the rare carnivore, *Eupleres goudotii*! Ted had unwittingly taken the first video ever of the toothless falanouc in the wild. Although related to the lemur-eating fossa, this small carnivore didn't eat vertebrates but pulled foot-long earthworms out of their tunnels and slurped them down like strands of spaghetti. We had never seen *Eupleres* in this park before, and could add a new mammal species to our biodiversity list. I was glad that Ted had chosen to spend his vacation with me in Madagascar.

John reminded us that it was Christmas Eve. The single malt he'd intended to celebrate with had already been sacrificed to the ancestors. However, he did have some pistachio pudding mix in his backpack, as well as five freeze-dried packets of astronaut turkey. Thus, our Maharira Christmas dinner consisted of Astronaut Turkey Delight with Mars Mashed Potatoes over rice with two teaspoons each of green pistachio pudding for dessert. We enjoyed the dinner but were still hungry. As if remembering something, Isabel jumped up and returned with a box that had been smushed into the bottom of her backpack.

"Merry Christmas," she announced. "It's an old family recipe. I made it back in Boston before I left on my trip." It was a dense, sweet fruitcake that we relished.

Afterward, John led us on a nighttime search for snakes, frogs, and chameleons in the swamp. As we sloshed down the stream with our headlamps blazing, I imagined that from a distance we might have passed for Santa and his reindeer.

John pointed to a vine growing across the stream. It had few leaves except for a fist-sized one in the center that looked like a white mitten hung on a clothesline.

"It's a chameleon, *Calumma oshaughnessy*." John pointed to the white form, now identifiable by its scaly eyes that were clenched shut, its clamp-like feet, and its tail curled in a spiral. "It's out here in the middle of the stream for protection against predators. If a snake or fossa starts to climb the vine, the chameleon will feel the movement and move to safety."

John explained why the chameleon was so white. Chameleons have different layers of pigment in their skin, with no color in the first. Below that are two layers of primary colors. If a chameleon looks green, the blue layer and the yellow layer are showing. When a chameleon is disturbed, it will switch to the fourth layer, which is made of melanin, and it turns black. At night, chameleons appear white because all the layers are turned off when they sleep.

Next, we found an inch-long chameleon that John identified as *Calumma nasuta*, the big-nosed chameleon. The male has a paddle-like nose, while the female has a delicate little nose and lays about six eggs a year, which isn't many for a chameleon. Some species lay up to fifty eggs at a time.

Then on a bare branch, blending in like a stick, was a skinny chameleon with huge flaps flattened to the sides of its head. It was the elephant-eared chameleon, *Calumma brevicornis*. During the day it was brightly colored, with iridescent blue legs, a red nose, and a body with vertical stripes.

By the time we returned to our tents, we'd seen seven different chameleons. Ted and I would always remember this as the Chameleon Christmas.

After Christmas, most of our team returned to the village of Ranomafana while John Cadle spent New Year's elsewhere. John wasn't finished with his research. He launched another expedition in the northern half of Ranomafana National Park near the distant village of Miaronony. He and his team of Emile, Georges, and Raphael walked all day to reach this pristine rainforest. That night they set up camp in the mountains at 3,600 feet.

After a week of catching frogs and snakes, John was sitting on the ground one afternoon writing up his field notes. The heat of the day had inspired Emile, Georges, and Raphael to take a nap in a tent thirty feet away. John was concentrating on his notes and never looked up to see the clouds roll in. He hadn't learned the lesson from Mount Maharira.

BAROOM.

The three men in the tent were shaken awake. A flash of searing light followed and the smell of burning canvas punctuated the air. Emile, Georges, and Raphael scrambled out of the tent and ran down the hill away from the lightning strike. As they ran, they suddenly remembered John. John was not running with them. They raced back to see John supine on the ground, eyes staring blankly.

"Is he dead?" Emile asked.

John later reported to me that he was temporarily paralyzed and unable to answer. Indeed, he wondered in his mind if he was dead.

"He must be dead," Georges said.

Then John blinked. He couldn't yet speak. The clouds opened and raindrops the size of pebbles began to pelt down. Realizing John was alive, the three men carried him into the tent. The lightning must have been attracted by the aluminum tent poles and traveled through the ground to where he'd been sitting. Inside, John regained his ability to speak and assured the others he was okay. The wind howled like a freight train and somewhere in the forest a tree fell with a gigantic crash. The ancestors seemed very angry.

John walked five hours down the mountain that day. Luckily, a car was waiting in the nearest village to take him to get help. It was only later that John realized he'd received third-degree burns from his waist to his toes. Once the shock subsided, the pain was indescribable. He sat in his tent for a week, his burned legs wrapped in salt compresses, and miraculously didn't get an infection. One leg was numb for almost a year, and some burn scars would be with him forever. Despite this, John returned to Madagascar in the rainy season the following year.

This time he brought two bottles of whiskey for the ancestors. Just in case.

Shortly after John underwent his unfortunate encounter with lightning, I had to return to Stony Brook and found myself immersed in teaching. I was also deep in my relationship with Jukka Jernvall. He was intrigued by me and interested in my science and what I'd accomplished in Madagascar. At first, I was wary about my feelings for Jukka. Amanda's father and I had gotten divorced thirteen years previously, and while I'd had relationships since then—mostly with other scientists, since that was the circle I moved in—they hadn't worked out. Could love really strike twice?

Jukka and I were married on May 8, 1993, on Long Island; not in a church, as neither of us were religious, but in the local library, a historic white wooden building with a steeple. To be married in a library made sense to us since we were both academics, my mother and two sisters were librarians, and Jukka's aunt was the librarian for the National Parliament of Finland. Since it was going to be a small wedding, we invited our families and a few close friends. We predicted that no one would come from Finland. Amanda was the maid of honor and looked beautiful with her blondish hair shining over her long, sea-blue gown. Jukka's best friend, John Hunter, was his best man. Elizabeth McGee, a graduate student in paleontology, helped decorate the house and the white Honda Civic, which was to be our getaway car.

Contrary to our expectations, Jukka's mother, sister, aunt, and Jukka's best friends from Finland all arrived with great fanfare. The Finns stayed a week shopping in New York City and then took a white stretch limousine to an inn close by the library the day before the wedding. My three brothers and two sisters and their spouses, as well as my mother and father, drove eight hours from western New York. Elwyn Simons, his wife Friderun, and their son Verne came up from North Carolina. Dave Haring also arrived from the Duke Primate Center and took photos. A Unitarian minister presided, an acoustic guitarist provided the music, and my brother Chris led a Buddhist chant.

Jukka and I had planned to honeymoon on Block Island off of Rhode Island but had forgotten to book the ferry. We were a bit embarrassed to go back home, since everyone would think we'd failed at taking a honeymoon. So we ended up spending a few nights at the Maiden Arms, an historic hotel in East Hampton, Long Island, an hour and a half from our house. Two weeks later, we went to Paris for a proper honeymoon, visiting the Latin Quarter, the Museum of Man, and the Living Museum of the Horse in Chantilly. Then Jukka boarded a plane for Helsinki and I got on a plane to Madagascar.

I had the feeling that this tricontinental marriage was going to be very romantic.

CHAPTER EIGHT

SOMETHING BIG

(1996)

EING MARRIED TO A scientist who spends long months doing research in the field is not easy. It's even harder when both spouses are scientists working in different areas of study. And in different continents, let alone countries. However, due to the long absences and dramatic reunions, this kind of relationship is never monotonous. Jukka came to Stony Brook when I taught during the spring semester, and I went to Helsinki during the "midnight sun" summers, while Jukka studied fossil teeth and the genetics of how teeth developed in mice.

The real test to the relationship came a few years after we'd gotten married, when Jukka accompanied me on an expedition to the southeastern rainforest of Madagascar. Nearly a decade previously, I'd visited Vondrozo to search for the greater bamboo lemur, and now I was returning to look for the white-collared brown lemur. I'd seen the animal on that first trip, but now I knew it was critically endangered and a survey was required to find out how many remained in their geographic range.

As we entered Vondrozo and drove down the street paved with stones and bones, I saw that not much had changed in ten years. I knew the routine. First, I had our authorization papers stamped at the mayor's office and then headed for the local Department of Water and Forests. The wooden building, not too fancy in 1986, was looking even more decrepit in 1996. The door was locked when we arrived.

Emile and Georges, our guides for this trip, disappeared to find *Le Chef* (the boss) as Jukka and I waited. Jukka was especially glad to be out of the car. Eight hours was an age to be trapped in a vehicle, especially when you had long legs.

I heard Georges' contagious laugh, and we saw him, Emile, and a Malagasy man moving down the hill toward us. This head of the Department of Water and Forests was much younger than the last *Chef*. When he took us into his office I noticed on the wall a yellowed 1960 map of Madagascar, which I recognized from the last time I was there.

"We are here to do surveys of a rare lemur called the white-collared brown lemur. You call it *Varika mauvo*, I think." I rummaged through my backpack and pulled out the stamped authorization papers.

"You want to go to Vevembe?" the young man said. "First, I must tell you I am not *Le Chef* but his assistant. He is not here today, he went to Farafangana. But you can go and start your project. I will keep a copy of your permits and give your authorizations to him. Randria, a local farmer, knows the forest well. When you get to the gate at Vevembe, ask the gatekeeper to find Randria for you."

The young man paused. "You came here before. With other *vasahas*."

I was surprised that someone recalled our visit in 1986.

"You don't remember me, do you?" the young man asked, smiling shyly.

"I'm sorry, I don't," I said.

He reached into his desk drawer and pulled out an old book with tattered pages and crinkled edges. I realized that I had once owned that book.

"I am the son of the President of Vondrozo. You came to our house and gave my father this book. I was twelve years old."

I took the book in my hands and turned the pages of bright green, red, and blue chameleons. Every page was worn thin from use. This young man must have read this book every day for ten years.

"I learned so much from this book. Thank you for this gift."

I didn't know what to say. Such a small gift had made such an impact. We stayed for a while to talk with him, and he pointed out in the book all the animals he'd seen.

In the morning, we drove north and then west up the escarpment to the forest called Vevembe at 1,500 feet. We found the farmer Randria, who suggested that we set up our camp in a large cleared area at the edge of a blackwater swamp filled with palm trees and *Pandanus* trees. That first night we heard the distinctive yipping of lemurs. At breakfast, we were thrilled to see that the sounds had emanated from white-collared brown lemurs, leaping one by one along the edge of the swamp. We counted seven individuals in the group.

That night, we sat around the campfire finishing our plates of rice and beans. We chatted about the lemurs, and which fish were found in the rivers nearby. Then I turned to Randria, and asked, "You've spent many years in this area. I'm wondering, have you seen something big?"

I always asked that whenever I was in a remote area, because deep in my heart I wanted to see a giant extinct lemur alive. And I remember that in this area ten years ago I had heard the story of the Rano-omby-be, the "big water cow."

Randria didn't answer me. I decided to drop the conversation and ask him again the next day. But in the morning, Randria was gone. He hadn't even discussed his departure with Emile or Georges. That evening, just in time for supper, Randria returned, again with no explanation. He dished up his rice and beans and ate quickly, put his plate in the blue bucket, and started talking.

"I did not want to lie. I have not seen 'something big,' so I went back to the village to talk to my uncle. Last night, my uncle confirmed that he has seen something big. Many times in a village near here."

"Can we go see your uncle?" I asked excitedly.

"No, you are white and the people will be afraid of you."

Finally, with some help from Emile and Georges, I convinced Randria to take us to that village the next day. Randria said that it would take three hours to get there, so I calculated that we should bring enough water for six hours, and some cheese, sardines, and bread for lunch. Maybe a chocolate bar, just in case.

Early the following morning, we set out on a trail inside the forest. Dawn was breaking and a flock of more than fifty screeching parrots flew overhead and disappeared into a fig tree. In front of us was a reedy swamp. The three Malagasy stepped into the water wearing their plastic sandals. Jukka and I waded in with our rubber boots, which quickly filled as the water rose over our knees. I glanced at Jukka, concerned, but he seemed to take this in stride.

Once we arrived on the other side of the swamp, we dried quickly as we hiked up a hill in the sun. The forest had given way to the vast grassland that covers all of western Madagascar. We had crossed the great divide from the east to the west of the country. The December sun burned overhead like an oven. Jukka's pale complexion was rapidly turning red.

"Are we nearly there?" I asked Emile, who asked Randria.

"He says it's not far," Emile reported.

By noon, my water bottle was almost empty. "Jukka, do you have any water left?"

Jukka's headshake indicated that he didn't. He turned to me. "How could you not have brought enough water? Water is a basic element of any expedition. . . ." He trailed off, too tired to lecture any further.

"Emile, ask Randria how much farther we have to travel," I said.

"Not far," was the answer.

In the distance we saw four men in felt hats like gangsters, herding about a dozen cattle. They had shotguns over their shoulders.

"Can we ask them for some water?" I suggested to Emile.

"*Dahalo*," Emile whispered. Cattle rustlers were not the kind of people you asked for a drink of water, and I didn't press the issue.

"At least they didn't kill us," I tried to joke after the four men passed by. I thought I heard Jukka mutter something like, "Perhaps better if they had."

It was nearly two in the afternoon now, and we were all dehydrated, overheated, and exhausted.

"Emile, ask him how much farther. . . , " I pleaded.

"Not far."

An hour later, clouds mercifully drifted over the sun and we stopped to rest at the top of a hill, looking out over the bleak, denuded landscape that seemed to stretch on forever.

"Pat, I don't think this is a good idea," Jukka said, his face flushed from sunburn. "This guide seems to be running us all over the place. I'm not sure he even has a destination in mind. And to find what, the Loch Ness Monster of Madagascar? We're serious scientists! This is crazy."

There was nothing I could say. Even if I could have come up with something in my defense, I didn't want to waste the breath to say it. I'd never been so thirsty in my life.

At five-thirty, after we'd been walking for nearly fourteen hours, Randria stopped and pointed down the hill to a village consisting of five huts. Smoke oozed from the roof of one of them. Randria instructed Jukka and me to wait while he, Emile, and Georges went down to his uncle's house to talk.

I grabbed Emile and spoke to him with desperation in my voice. "Emile, I know how charming you are. I have seen you with women. Please use all that charm and get the woman of the house to boil us some water, lots of water."

Emile nodded and the group left for the house with the smoking roof while Jukka and I stayed in the bushes. After ten minutes, Emile retrieved us. As we passed through the bramble gate and entered the bare dirt yard, we were accosted by a boy of about fifteen years. He tried to speak but the sounds just gurgled in his throat. Instead, he smiled a greeting and pointed to the door of the hut. Jukka had to stoop low as he entered. A woman stood in front of a fire over which large aluminum pots full of water hung over the fire, heating up. She gestured for us to sit.

The hut was very simple, with a hand-woven reed mat covering the dirt floor. Jukka and I collapsed on it as gracefully as possible. Since there were no windows, the smoke from the fire made it difficult to see or breathe. I could make out baskets holding the family's belongings in the corners of the room. Above our heads, firewood was stacked on a wooden plank balanced over the cross beams. A toddler clutched her mother's skirt, whimpering. Another daughter, about eight years old, appeared to be mute like her brother and her arms were covered with scabies. She handed Jukka and me tin cups of water, which we sipped as quickly as we could without burning our throats.

Emile told us that Maro, the wife of Randria's uncle, had had nine children, five of whom had died before they were two years old. These three were the only children who survived, except for her oldest daughter who lived next door with her new husband. Randria's uncle would be arriving from the fields soon. However, there wasn't enough food for all of us to eat.

I gave Maro some money from my pocket, and she sent her son to buy food from the next village. Ravenous, Jukka and I sipped cup after cup of water, thanking Maro after each cup, and nodding for more when asked. Then Jukka slumped to the ground, his eyes red and weeping from the smoke. Finally, the boy came back with two cups of rice and a live chicken. Maro stepped outside and we heard the chicken's squawking cease. The scrawny corpse went in the cooking pot.

An elderly man with an orange, beige, and blue plaid blanket tossed over his shoulder entered the hut. He shook each of our hands in turn, and sat down on the east side of the hut near Maro. She set the plates out one by one with equal portions of rice and chicken. With spoons made of wooden sticks flattened at the end, we eagerly scooped up the food.

Then Randria's uncle addressed us. "You have come a long way to discuss what I have seen. Yes, I have seen 'something big' in a pond nearby."

"How big?" I wanted to get specifics as quickly as possible.

"As big as a car."

My eyebrows rose in surprise. Some giant lemurs, *Archaeo-indris*, were as big as a gorilla, but this size took primates out of the realm of possibility. "What color is it?"

"*Maisena*." Dark.

"*Maity*?" Black? I tried to clarify his answer.

"No, *maisena*."

That made sense, as no big animal that lives in the water is truly black, even the hippopotamus.

"Did it have hair? A tail or ears?"

"No tail or ears. I mostly saw its back as it came out of the water to breathe and then dove to the bottom of the pond."

The Rano-omby-be that had been described to me ten years ago had ears that stood up on the top of its head. Because it breathed air, this big animal must be a mammal, or maybe a giant crocodile.

"Is it a *voay*?"

Randria's uncle laughed and told us that he had seen many crocodiles in this region, but this animal was not a crocodile. It ate water plants and slept in a cave near the pond. He had seen it five or six times in his life, the first time when he was ten years old and the last time in October of this year.

"Two months ago?" I exclaimed, my mind racing. "Can you show me where this pond is?"

"Yes, tomorrow morning we can go see it. But now it is time to go to sleep. You and your husband can stay in our guest hut."

Jukka and I were shown to a thatched adobe mud hut. We were glad to get away from the smoke, but after a few minutes we yearned for a fire. As hot as the daytime had been, at night the temperatures plunged. But this guesthouse had no fire-place, and we had no matches anyway. Soon, it became appar-ent that the empty hut was already occupied. Rats chased each other over the roof beams. Our flashlights revealed spiders and cockroaches that scrambled to get under the mat on the floor. Mosquitoes that surely carried malaria, filariasis, and dengue

An aye-aye (*Daubentonia madagascariensis*) at Duke Lemur Center. This one is the offspring of the one I captured in 1987. Photo by Noel Rowe, 2012.

Vondrozo, 1986.

From left: David Meyers, Deb Overdorff, Emile Rajaerison, me, Patrick Daniels, Bedo, Bernhard Meier, and Loret Rasabo searching for bamboo lemurs in Ranomafana forest, 1986. Photo in RNP archives.

Meeting the elders at Amboimiera, the northernmost village of Ranomafana National Park, during the park's delineation. With Emile Rajiarison (wearing the cap to my left), Loret Rasabo (with binoculars), and Edmond from the Department of Water and Forests (on my right). Photo by Patrick Daniels, 1987.

Searching for lemurs in Ranomafana forest, 1987.

Crossing the bridge above the Namarona River to Ranomafana forest. Photo by David Meyers, 1987.

Lon Kightlinger and his health team in a remote village—one of our first steps to winning the trust and hearts of the local people. Photo by David Haring, 1990.

John Cadle, Loret Rasabo, and I at the campsite on Mt. Maharira. Photo by David Haring, 1992.

1986, the year I arrived in Ranomafana. Photo by Patrick Daniels.

With Amanda in 1989, discussing lemurs at dinner at the old research cabin.

Chameleon over the stream, Christmas Eve, Mount Maharira. Photo by David Haring, 1992.

The frog discovered in the cave at Mount Maharira. Photo by David Haring, 1992.

The golden bamboo lemur (*Hapalemur aureus*), Ranomafana National Park. Photo by Noel Rowe, 2013.

The mysterious new lemur from Kalambatritra Reserve, later named *Lepilemur wrightae*. Photo by Desire Randriarista, 2005.

Greater bamboo lemur
(*Prolemur simus*).
Ranomafana National Park.
Photo by Noel Rowe.

The skulls of the giant lemur (*Megaladapis edwardsi*) and the ring-tailed lemur (*Lemur catta*), a living lemur the size of a small fox. Photo taken by Noel Rowe at Centre ValBio, Ranomafana, 2012.

Milne-Edwards' sifaka (*Propithecus edwardsi*) ready to leap. Photo by Jukka Jernvall.

Milne-Edwards' sifaka "kicking back" in a tree in Ranomafana. Photo by Nitin Kasturi.

Above: The inauguration of LovaBe Hall with Dada Lira, village musician, and his daughter. Photo by David Haring, 2003.

Right: Professor Elwyn Simons and elders at the village next to Christmas River, east of Ilakakabe, before the ceremony to ask the ancestors to bless our expedition. Photo by Patricia Wright, 2008.

Top, Left: Amanda, Arianna, Miguel, and Issan at John F. Kennedy airport, 2012. Photo by Patricia C. Wright, 2012.

Top, Right: My Commandeur Medal of Honor. Photo by Noel Rowe, 2012.

Right: Ali Yapaglucio, architect for NamanaBe Hall, Centre ValBio, and I discuss the construction, on the balcony of LovaBe hall. Photo by Noel Rowe, 2011.

NamanaBe Hall, Centre ValBio. Photo by Desire Randriarisata, 2011.

NamanaBe Hall, Centre ValBio at night. Photo by James Ewing, 2011.

buzzed in our ears. Jukka fumbled in his daypack and triumphantly pulled out a red plastic raincoat, the kind that can be scrunched into a pouch. When we huddled close together, we were able to cover ourselves completely. Although Jukka fell asleep, I remained awake, my mind churning with thoughts about the mysterious creature that lurked in the pond.

At first daylight, Jukka and I climbed to the top of a hill near the village. Since it had been dark by the time we'd arrived the night before, we didn't know what our surroundings looked like. The landscape was filled with streams and rivers reflecting the dawn. Interspersed among them were patches of forest and large ponds and lakes, stretching to the horizon. Two of the rivers were quite wide, making me think that the mysterious creature could have migrated from elsewhere. If it were a hippopotamus, it would have to leave the water to graze. I began to look for signs of a mammal along the banks: munched grass, footprints, or droppings. There was nothing.

Back at the hut of Randria's uncle, steaming bowls of soup rice made for a satisfying breakfast. Then the uncle took us to the pond where he'd seen "something big" in October. We walked west along a path cresting a hill. Below was a pond with a large channel that exited and entered. It was about forty yards across and a hundred yards long, with a large boulder at the entrance from the east. Randria's uncle took us to the northern edge of the pond, explaining that it was *fady* to go on the other side. When I asked if anyone had ever gone in the pool, he shook his head.

"The water is very cold and very deep. Also, we don't want to make this animal angry. It brings us good luck."

The surface of the pond was calm, and although we stayed for nearly an hour, we didn't see any sign of life.

Before we left the village to walk back to camp, Randria's uncle made an unusual request.

"There is one thing that we would like you to do. We are worried because the government requires us to provide photos to get our identification cards. But we don't have a camera and are far from any town. Can you take our photos? If we don't have identification cards, we could be arrested. We need to carry the photos all the way to Vondrozo to get the cards issued by the end of the year.

We agreed, and the members of the family went into the hut to get ready to have their pictures taken. When they emerged, I was stunned. Gone were their rags, and their faces were scrubbed and their hair combed. The son was dressed in an oversized gray suit jacket over a white button-down shirt and dark pants. The older daughter wore a blue taffeta dress with white ribbons braided into her hair. A red-and-gold *lambda* was draped over Maro's skirt, and a white *lambda* over her shoulder. Even Randria's uncle looked dapper in a straw hat.

Understanding the importance to the family, Jukka carefully snapped a photo of each person. We explained that we'd send the prints by bush taxi to Vondrozo and Randria would deliver the photos the next time he visited.

We shook hands and bowed to each family member, and then prepared for our journey back to Vevembe. Jukka had pulled maps out of his backpack and insisted there was a better way to return, along an old road built by the French in the 1930s. Walking down this road was like going back in time.

We passed the ruins of villages abandoned decades before. Overhead were telephone poles that had long ago fallen into disuse, an occasional limp wire left over from those that had been stolen to sell in the Tana market. How different Madagascar must have been forty years previously, before the revolution!

Fortunately, the day was cloudy, masking the sun's heat. We had full water bottles and from trees by the roadside we picked red jujubes, Emile's favorite fruit, which he called "jojoby apples." Then we came to a broad, dark river with huge trees arching over the tannin-filled waters.

"This is the Sarabidy River," Emile said. "It flows into the Manampatrana River and then down to the Indian Ocean. Crocodiles live in here."

Lying across the vast river was a skeleton of a bridge, just a lattice of iron beams. The wooden planks had long since deteriorated or been stolen. I had a secret: Despite my many years of experience in the rainforests of the Amazon and Madagascar, I was scared of heights. And this bridge was two stories high.

"Come on, Pat," Jukka said, holding a hand out to me.

I tried not to look down, or think, or do anything but inch over that very long bridge. We all made it, and the crocodiles went hungry that day.

Once across the bridge, we stopped so that my heart could recover and also to consult the map. It appeared that we were within an hour of our campsite in Vevembe.

Jukka studied the map further. "Look here." He pointed to an area south of Amparafitra, the village where Randria's uncle lived. It was a network of rivers starting from the Ihosy River and draining into the Midongy du sud Massif, east of Kalambatritra Reserve. Bezavona, the town where the Rano-omby-be had been seen, was in this vicinity.

I thought about what kind of creature could live in this river drainage system. It could the Malagasy hippopotamus, a species that was thought to have crossed the Mozambique Channel more than ten thousand years ago and went extinct less than a thousand years ago. From its many subfossils it appeared to be small, the size of the current-day pygmy hippopotamus. Or the creature could be a manatee, although the species that survives today in Africa is on the western coast of the continent. Or it could be a Steller's Sea Cow, a similar marine mammal that had gone extinct in the late 1700s. Whatever this creature was, I had to find it.

"Jukka," I said. "We have to go to Kalambatritra."

Jukka was silent for a moment. I imagined that he was reviewing in his mind the slog through the swamp, the hours-long trek across the grasslands without water, and the chilly, vermin-infested hut we'd stayed in last night.

"I love you, Pat, I really do," he said. "But let's not think about any further expeditions until tomorrow." And he put away the map. For the next month, we searched the forests for the white-collared lemurs and found five groups, with an average group size of seven, and home ranges of twenty hectares.

We never did get to go to Kalambatritra on that trip. In fact, Jukka didn't return to Madagascar until 2003. But the Rano-omby-be, the mysterious creature, the "something big," would continue to haunt my dreams for years.

CHAPTER NINE

THE GREAT BAMBOO
CONUNDRUM

(1997)

IN THE WORLD of taxonomic classification, it's common for species names to change once further information is discovered about the animal's relationship to others. For example, the name for the white-collared brown lemur (*Eulemur albocollaris*) that I searched for with Jukka in 1996 was changed to the gray-headed brown lemur (*Eulemur cinericeps*) in 2008.

In 1998, the greater bamboo lemur's classification was altered from *Hapalemur simus* to *Prolemur simus*. The taxonomist Colin Groves proclaimed that the teeth were totally different from other lemurs, and that such a dramatic difference meant this species had to be a different genus. What remained the same, though, was that the greater bamboo lemur continued to be one of the most endangered species of lemur in Madagascar, as it is today. *Prolemur simus* was once abundant over a broad geographic area in the north and northwest, according to subfossil findings. For many years, only two populations were known to exist: one in Ranomafana National Park and the other in Kianjavato, thirty miles east of Ranomafana, where they were unprotected. Their home range was substantial, over two hundred fifty acres, three times larger than the sifakas' territory, and five times greater than the golden bamboo lemurs' territory. *Prolemur simus* had a specialized diet, eating only a few kinds of giant bamboo, and then solely the pith inside the bamboo trunks. Giant bamboo tended to grow along the banks of large rivers, where the soil was most fertile, so that was also the first land that farmers targeted to slash and burn. As those areas became deforested, it grew harder for the lemur groups to find each other in order to reproduce.

During the 1990s, a few greater bamboo lemurs were kept in zoos in Europe, but in the early years they did not breed in captivity. Then, in 1994, the female in a pair of greater bamboo lemurs at the Paris Zoo died, and her mate stopped eating. Afraid that the male would also die, the Zoo placed him with another greater bamboo lemur pair. Some experts predicted that the two males would try to kill each other, but instead both males attempted to mate with the female. Within five months, the first captive-born offspring of this species came into the world. The method was replicated elsewhere, and since then one greater bamboo lemur offspring has been born nearly every year where two males competed for the attention of a single female.

Now that breeding colonies were a viable option, it was time to start one in Madagascar. The Madagascar Fauna Group, a consortium of international and national conservation groups aiming to preserve the country's endemic species, had upgraded a zoological center called Parc Ivoloina in Toamasina on the east coast. The Parc determined that they could support a breeding colony. Then, a third group of *simus* was spotted in Karianga, in the southeastern rainforest near Vondrozo. However, they were being hunted by farmers and the forest in which they lived was fewer than twelve acres and became smaller during every burning season. I volunteered to organize an expedition to obtain six greater bamboo lemurs from this area for Madagascar's first breeding colony.

This time I was the leader of the expedition. I invited Elwyn Simons, his son Verne, and Amanda to come. Loret, Richard, and the rest of our group set out for Karianga, with three large dog kennels packed into two Land Cruisers. Amanda had graduated *cum laude* from Boston University with a major in International Relations and a minor in French and was taking a year off to decide her next steps. Verne was about to enter Duke University as a freshman. Richard Ramandrapihaona, the young villager who accompanied us in Sahavondronana in 1991, worked with us at Ranomafana National Park. He and Loret carried the capture guns and anesthetic darts.

Our first problem was the Manampatrana River, which at thirty yards across is one of the widest in all Madagascar. The road ended at the riverbank, and there was no bridge. Désiré Randrianarisata (who was called Dede and was the lead driver) exited the car—as did the rest of us. My eyes followed the graceful black shape of a crested drongo flying across the water to what appeared to be a tanker on the other side of the river.

"Dede, what is that?" I asked.

A grin spread over Dede's face as he recognized the *bac*, a hand-drawn ferry. It consisted of a rusted metal platform on pontoons and a long rope that stretched all the way across the river, moved by a man pulling on this thick rope hand over hand. It took over half an hour for the ferryman to reach us. He anchored the *bac* and Dede drove onto the platform. A dozen children watched as the ferryman labored, and clapped and cheered when our two vehicles reached the opposite shore.

Once we arrived in Karianga, we performed the usual rite of visiting the mayor's office and the local Department of Water and Forests to get our permits stamped. Our permits allowed us to capture six greater bamboo lemurs. Then we proceeded west to the site where the greater bamboo lemurs had been seen a year ago. As darkness fell, we unpacked and set up camp just off the road in the grasslands outside of the forest.

"Oof," Loret grunted as he moved Elwyn's suitcase from the roof of the car. Loret was big for a Malagasy and strong, but he strained under the weight. "This is a big suitcase, *Dadabe*," he said to Elwyn, using the Malagasy word of respect for grandfathers.

"What's in there, Elwyn?" I teased. "Do you have a change of clothes for every meal?"

"You're too young to know," Elwyn responded gruffly.

That night in my tent, as I snuggled into my sleeping bag, I heard a rumbling. Was it a tree falling? An earthquake? I pulled on my fieldpants and dashed outside. I saw Dede and Loret running toward Elwyn's tent. They slowed down when they realized what was happening. Elwyn was using the generator that had been in his suitcase to blow up a huge air mattress that could fit a king bed. It completely covered the bottom of Elwyn's four-man tent. I shook my head, not wanting to know any more.

In the morning, we trekked to a forest thicket about twenty minutes from the campsite. Elwyn and I sat on a hill across from the copse to watch for any escaping lemurs, while inside the thicket Loret, Richard, and Dede stalked the animals. In the middle of the morning I decided to head back to camp to get some more water. When I was twenty yards away, I instinctively stopped, feeling that I wasn't alone. Pricked up in the grass, near the road, were two gray ears with white ear tufts.

I stood stock still as the greater bamboo lemur crossed the road, speeding to a gallop halfway through. A second lemur followed, then another, in single file. I counted fifteen, sixteen. A younger one scampered ahead of the others. Twenty, twenty-one. The group size ended up being twenty-six individuals. The biggest group at Ranomafana had only eleven. This was very good news, indeed.

With this information I redirected our capture team, and they darted three males and three females. We gently laid their sleeping forms on a tarp for measurements. The biggest adults weighed between 5.5 and 11 pounds and were very thin. As each lemur began to rouse from anesthesia, Elwyn took charge. Holding the lemur in his arms like a baby, Elwyn delicately dispensed water from an eyedropper onto each lemur's dense fur, and let the awakening animal groom off the liquid. He had also lined each of the three large dog kennels with fluffy gray Turkish towels from his suitcase.

"They have a long way to go, so they have to be as comfortable as possible," he reasoned.

Elwyn and I instructed Loret and Richard to cut a large
amount of bamboo while Verne and Amanda cradled the
awakening lemurs. Once the lemurs were inside the kennels,
we fed them bamboo stalks through the metal bars. All of
them accepted food except for a subadult male who crouched
miserably in the back of the kennel. We kept feeding the animals once we'd decamped and were back on the road, but ran
out of bamboo five hours into the trip. Fortunately, we discovered that these notoriously fussy eaters would also consume
stalks from roadside ginger plants. When we got to the coastal
town of Farafangana, we toured the market and bought green
beans, carrots, cucumbers, and spinach-like leaves, and the
lemurs (even the subadult male) seemed to like those, too.

It took two more days before we reached Parc Ivoloina,
where the lemurs settled into their new homes. Parc Ivoloina,
funded by the Madagascar Fauna Group and Duke University
was a zoo with huge cages, all outdoors. The cages housed
about seventy-five lemurs including black-and-white ruffed
lemurs, white-faced brown lemurs, and gray bamboo lemurs.
Because the park was located in a rainforest climate and the
right species of bamboo grew nearby, we figured the bamboo
lemurs would do well. And indeed they did. One of the greater
bamboo lemur females gave birth to an infant within a year.

Having a breeding colony of greater bamboo lemurs in Madagascar was a step toward conservation, but the strategy to
save them from extinction needed to be more comprehensive.

Luckily, our knowledge of the greater bamboo lemur started to increase over the years, offering possible solutions.

One greater bamboo lemur set, the TALA (*"Talatakely"* means Little Tuesday) group in Ranomafana National Park, has provided all of the information we know about the species. This was the group that I identified in the 1980s but was unable to study. They skillfully eluded me, using a number of tricks, including the "group scatter," "hide above a thick branch for eight hours without moving," and "see Pat and race two miles at top speed to the other side of the territory." By mapping the bamboo leaves and shoots they left behind, I could outline their territory, but I could never follow them from dawn to dusk as I could the other lemurs.

But in 1993, Chia Tan, my graduate student at Stony Brook, became interested in them. Born in Taiwan, Chia had immigrated at the age of eleven to a poor neighborhood in Los Angeles. She habituated the group to human presence and for six years she successfully followed the TALA group in Ranomafana National Park. A researcher, Ny Hamashita, studied the group's jaw mechanics and how they are able to crush the bamboo. Eileen Larney documented their vocalizations and their intricate communication calls. Jean Aimee, a Malagasy student from the University of Antananarivo, observed how they raised their infants.

One of the biggest discoveries made during this time was in the way the greater bamboo lemur evades predation and what it means for male and female roles in the group. This species of lemur tend to bite the bamboo stalks where they're softest and juiciest, which is often a meter from the ground. And, unlike other lemurs, *simus* is a "central place forager," which means the group doesn't move around browsing from tree to tree like other primates, but stays in one place eating bamboo for about ten days. Then the group will move to the far side of their territory to eat bamboo at that site for a further ten days.

This feeding strategy has its downside: chewing with can-opener teeth for forty-five minutes through the trunks of giant bamboo is a noisy activity, as is communicating with one another, which makes them easy prey. Also, they leave behind a large amount of litter—not only discarded pieces of bamboo but their feces, bright green fibrous pellets that smell like fresh-mown hay. Although this can be a signal to other bamboo lemurs to stay away, it also attracts predators like the fossa, a catlike viverrid related to the civet who is as at ease in trees as on the forest floor. Another predator is Henst's goshawk, the largest raptor in Madagascar after the fishing eagle.

What the greater bamboo lemur developed in order to counteract these predators—regretably, in my opinion—is a strong and unequivocal male dominance. While the females chew open the trunks of the bamboo, the males patrol for predators. If a fossa appears, the group individually scatters in multiple directions, hiding singly and not moving for hours. If the predator is a raptor, the *simus* drop to the forest floor, camouflaged against the leaf litter, and slink off in slow motion one by one. Naturally, the patroling males have the power in the group, taking bamboo away from the yearlings and subadults after the females open the trunks. In primate language, this behavior signals dominance. The males also determine when and where the groups move next. This is unlike all other lemur species, where the female is dominant.

The breeding dynamics of the TALA group remained stable for almost two decades. From 1986 to 2004 the group size hovered between seven and eleven individuals, with two breeding females and a few adult males. The females bred like clockwork in May and gave birth in early November. But one day in December 2004, both of the adult males in the group disappeared. There were now only five individuals: two adult females, two yearlings, and one female subadult. We thought that the males would return during the breeding season, but none showed up and no infants were born in 2005. Even though the females scent-marked their territory and gave communication calls, the males did not show up during the 2006 breeding season either.

Then, at the end of April 2006, the TALA group left the forest where they had lived for twenty years, traversed a bridge over the Namorona River, crossed the National Highway, and headed east. The lead female had a radio collar, so the group was able to be tracked. In all my years of studying primates, I had never heard of a group migrating together. In other lemurs, dispersal from a group is usually accomplished by one eligible adult male, or an adult female taking off solo to find a new group, or a subadult leaving with a close relative. But this family safari was unusual.

The next morning, the group found the Ambatolahy Dimy Group, a *simus* family living in a bamboo area on the edge of Ranomafana National Park. We'd been following this group on and off since 2000. In 2003, the family of five had diminished to two animals, a mother and daughter. They'd been without males for three years. The TALA group stayed with them for less than a week before continuing on their quest. They backtracked west to the top of a mountain with a TV transmission tower, and then north, following the streams. In total, they must have covered more than ten miles squared, leaving behind bamboo detritus and scent markings. After two months of their "walk-about" journey, they'd circled back to their original territory, their journey to find males apparently a failure. Then, in July, a large male showed up in the group and stayed. And on December 17, 2006, an infant *Prolemur simus* was born. The following year, on October 18, a second infant was born. The TALA group had momentarily been revived, but their survival is never certain.

After seventy biodiversity surveys over the past twenty-five years, the known *Prolemur simus* population has grown to three groups in Kianjavato, one group in Karianga, three groups in Ranomafana National Park (one of which my Stony Brook University graduate student Summer Arrigo-Nelson found in 2004), one group north of Ranomafana (discovered in 2000), and the Ambatolahy Dimy Group on the edge of Ranomafana. In the beginning of 2007, the total was three sites, eight groups, and fifty individuals—keeping the greater bamboo lemur well on the brink of extinction.

That year, Russ Mittermeier, primatologist and president of the Margot Marsh Biodiversity Foundation, awarded Stony Brook funding to search for *Prolemur simus*. My graduate student Rachel Jacobs began to survey all the areas of past sightings. Two months later, she reported that the Karianga group had died out due to slash-and-burn farming. However, she had found a group of twenty-eight next to the village of Ivato, west of Karianga, where it was *fady* to hunt them. The three groups in Kianjavato, a total of thirty-five animals, remained intact. Around that time, German conservationist Rainer Dolch and a team from the Malagasy NGO Mitsinjo sighted three large groups of over twenty individuals at the edge of a swamp near Andasibe, halfway between Antananarivo and Toamasina. This was the farthest north this species had been sighted alive. Then, Tony King from the Aspinall Foundation with a team of Malagasy researchers discovered more groups in that region. Still, the fact remains that surveys of more than 400 miles squared had turned up fewer than five hundred individuals.

In addition to deforestation, climate change was affecting the greater bamboo lemur population. Judging from the long-term rainfall record for Ranomafana National Park, the trend was toward a longer dry season. If the weather stayed dry too long, the bamboo trunks that *Prolemur simus* relied on became woody and inedible. Streams could also turn into a trickle, depriving the lemurs of water. The disappearance of one stream could mean the disappearance of lemurs.

We began an action plan to reforest giant bamboo along rivers to connect the primary forest to the isolated forest fragments that contained bamboo lemurs. But that method was slow. In 2012, we decided to translocate three lemurs, two females, and a male by rescuing them from a burning forest fragment. Just capturing them on that steep forest was nerve-wracking, but we accomplished it. We drove the animals in dog kennels for ten kilometers along bumpy, slippery clay roads to the research station. We first weighed, measured, and collared each lemur at the Centre ValBio Research Station and named them Christine, Josiane, and Misy. Then we released the three into a five-yard-cubed enclosure made with chicken wire and filled with bamboo. The three lemurs immediately started feeding.

We had no idea if the resident mother and daughter would ever find these caged lemurs. However, they must have heard the strangers' calls or smelled them. The next day, the resident father and daughter arrived and jumped onto the top of the cage. The air was filled with shrieks and growls and it didn't sound like the resident group liked the strangers. After an hour, the resident group settled down and sat together grooming ten yards from the enclosure. I decided we should open the cage.

At first, Christina, Josiane, and Misy didn't leave and ate the bamboo inside the cage. The father and daughter continued to call and investigate through the wires. Then as if she was gliding down the red carpet, Josiane walked with dignity along a piece of bamboo and out of the cage. She glanced only once at me and jumped into the trees. Christine emerged next with a running start and finally, hesitantly, the young male, Misy.

There followed a loud swaying of branches, and jumping and chattering, as the lemurs chased one another. I held my breath. Would these few smell the desperation of extinction? Did they know how few of them there were in the whole world? Could they understand that their romance might be essential for the survival of greater bamboo lemurs on Earth. The resident group was chasing the strangers and I feared a bloody fight. But no, by the time the sun was setting the two groups were sleeping about twenty meters apart.

The morning brought more chasing and I worried the matchmaking wasn't going to work. Misy, the male moved a hundred yards away, but the two females stuck together for several days. Misy eventually moved farther away, and we followed the radio collar. After ten days, he left the range of our receiver. Our experiment in translocation would only be considered a success when an infant was born. Since Misy was out of the picture, and from what we learned in the Paris Zoo, the best plan was to go back to rescue more males.

CHAPTER TEN

FLYING ANGELS

(1999)

A S MY EFFORTS to save the greater bamboo lemur continued, I urgently needed to help with sifakas. Mireya Mayor, one of my graduate students at Stony Brook, suspected that for over a hundred years four sifaka species had been disguised under the name of one, named for the halo of fluffy fur around its face. At the time, the evidence for separate species was circumstantial, based on minimal observations of the animals. It was known that Perrier's sifaka, which had black fur, was found in the far northeast of the country, as was the silky sifaka, which had white fur. The diademed sifaka, which was orange, black, and white like a calico cat, was found in the north-to-mideast. And the Milne-Edwards' sifaka, which had black fur with a white saddle, was found in the mid-to-southeast, including Ranomafana National Park. The best way to find out if there were indeed four different species was to catch a representative of each, measure them, take blood samples, and compare their DNA.

Mireya and I decided to look for the white sifaka, also called the silky sifaka, which lived in the high elevation rainforests of Marojejy Reserve in the northeast. They are often called "the ghosts of the forest" because of their coloring and the way they can be seen flitting from tree to tree. The animal was first documented in the West in 1871 by French naturalist Alfred Grandidier, who at first thought it was an albino variant of another species. Then, Ian Tattersall, a lemur expert from the American Museum of Natural History, described it as *Propithecus diadema candidus* in his 1982 book. The truth was that there was little information about the silky sifaka before our attempt to discover more in the late 1990s.

Collecting the first data ever on the silky sifaka would be a difficult task, but I knew that if any of my students were up to the challenge it would be Mireya Mayor. Raised in Miami by a single mother who had fled Castro's Cuba, Mireya had overcome her share of difficulties to find success. She'd been a straight-A student at the University of Miami and a cheerleader for the Miami Dolphins. She'd also starred on a Spanish-language soap opera. But it was a trip as a research assistant following monkeys in Guyana, South America, that made her decide to become a primatologist.

We'd be accompanied on this trip by an American journalist named Peter Tyson, who'd been commissioned by the PBS television program *NOVA* to imbed with our team and provide real-time commentary and photos of the expedition online. At the last minute, an American undergraduate named Mike Kraus from Washington University in St. Louis also joined us.

The rest of the team consisted of students from the University of Antananarivo; our guides, including Loret and a Marojejy guide named Désiré; and porters.

We all gathered at the foot of Mount Marojejy to begin our journey. This part of northeastern Madagascar was famous for its vanilla, clove, and cinnamon plantations. We could smell the fragrances in the air and see the thick-leaved vanilla plants with their chocolate-brown pods clinging to the trees.

We were almost ready to go, except that our baggage needed to be weighed to decide payment for the porters. The heap of forty-two items contained Peter's camera and computer equipment in metal cases, gunnysacks filled with pots and other cooking implements, duffels with green tents and blue tarps, a dart gun, and a liquid nitrogen tank that needed to be carried upright. With a metal scale, Désiré weighed each item and distributed it to the porters. He finally gave me the verdict: "The total they want for carrying these bags is 3.2 million Malagasy francs."

I looked at him in disbelief. The sum was nearly three times what I had budgeted. "Can you negotiate?" I asked.

Désiré talked to the barefoot, unsmiling men and turned back to me. "That is the final price, Madame Patricia. These men live by transporting vanilla on their shoulders. They won't come down on prices."

I had no choice, so I agreed, and the twenty-two porters hoisted the baggage on their backs and trotted up the trail. We wouldn't see either them or our bags until later that day when we reached what was called Camp II at 2,400 feet. The rest of us started our climb on a trail lined with ferns and gnarled trees decorated with vines and white orchids. At one point, I stopped to pick an isopod off the forest floor. It was a three-inch-long pill bug that looked like an ancient Jurassic insect, a miniature armored dinosaur. It rolled up tight in the palm of my hand, as large as a golf ball made out of malachite, that deep green stone from Central Africa. I placed it off the trail in the leaf litter and moved on.

Mike, the American undergraduate, fell into step beside me. "Are there leeches in this forest?" he asked. "I heard that sometimes they can fall into your eyes from above. Is that true?"

Knowing that descriptions of leeches never matched their wriggling reality, I reassured Mike that leeches were small, usually came out after it had been raining, and wouldn't be much of a problem.

"I'm going to wear my raincoat and my rain pants," Mike decided. "Then they can't get me." And he dropped behind to put on his blue raingear.

About two hours into the journey, I noticed that Peter was having some trouble. He was carrying his computer since he didn't trust the porters with such delicate equipment, and had slipped from second in line to sixth. He was also limping. Earlier, he'd confided to me that he was wearing new hiking boots, which wasn't a good idea for a steep hike like this. Soon he'd fallen behind Mike, who was sweating profusely from his impermeable raincoat and pants.

"Maybe you should take off your raingear," I suggested to Mike.

"I'm fine, really," he puffed. "Don't worry about me."

Apparently, Mike was more concerned about leeches than overheating. When we got to Camp I, which consisted of a few bungalows, I managed to convince him to change his clothes, which may have saved his life.

By the time we reached Camp II, Peter could hardly walk. He didn't join us for our dinner of rice and beans and burnt rice-water, so Mireya and I took a first aid kid into his tent. His feet were red and swollen, with pus oozing from some of the blisters. Using skills she'd learned from her mother, a nurse, Mireya dressed and bandaged his feet.

"Do you have oral antibiotics?" she asked. "You should start those immediately."

"I have some, but I'm sure I'll be fine tomorrow," Peter said.

"Maybe." Mireya shot me a look over Peter's head.

At dawn we were able to see just how imposing our surroundings were. Mount Marojejy towered above us at 7,035 feet, as steep as an Alp. A little further down from our campsite was a bare granite cliff with a waterfall plunging over it. Small yellow wagtail birds dipped into the water before soaring over trees that were bent into graceful sculptures from the wind. I felt like an eagle, perched above the rest of the world.

Peter's feet were still swollen but he was able to sit up and type his daily report into his computer. "I need to dispatch this," he said. "Plus, I need a photo to go along with the text."

It was clear that Peter wasn't in any shape to go outside to take a picture, so Mireya volunteered. As the rest of us watched with our breaths held, she walked along the glassy rocks near the stream to get a good shot of the waterfall. One time, she almost slipped, but caught herself with a back flip. "Lucky on that one!" she exclaimed, holding up the intact camera. Her cheerleading skills were certainly coming in handy.

After a breakfast of coffee and rice pudding, Mireya and I with our guides started to cut a trail up the mountain. Gray-green lichen clung to the granite and dense moss hung from the tall, twisted trees. The entire mountainside was dotted with the bright pink blossoms of the princess tree, a Malagasy version of cherry blossom. Every twenty-five yards we placed Day-Glo orange strips of flagging tape to officially mark the trail.

The branches above me swished and my eyes darted toward the movement. A soft grunting betrayed that it had come from a brown lemur, and soon we were able to spot brown tails swinging back and forth like pendulums. Several bushy, vanilla-colored faces peered down at us. I recognized *Eulemur fulvus albifrons*, the white-fronted brown lemur, a subspecies of the brown lemur that is only found in the northeastern rainforest. There were ten individuals: four males, four females, and two smaller juvenile males. We had just sighted our first lemurs in Marojejy.

We returned to camp, eager to tell the others about our discovery, and found that not only was Peter still unable to stand on his feet, but now Mike was down, too. He'd spent the day sweating and delirious in his tent, convinced that he had malaria. Mireya took his temperature.

"It's only 100 degrees, so I don't think you're in danger," she said. "But you should keep drinking fluids."

Mike murmured something unintelligible.

The next day, Mireya and I began walking the transect we'd cut the day before. Even with the trail marked we had to look at our feet for every step. We stopped when we heard the sound of branches swishing. Seven large white lemurs peered down on us from ten feet above.

"Oh, how beautiful!" I gasped in astonishment.

One of the silky sifakas had a bright pink face, while another had a beige face with black on its chin. Each one had pure white fur from its crown to the tip of its tail. They stared at us for a moment, as if in disbelief, and then made the "Sifak!" alarm call. Like acrobats in retreat, they leaped into the forest, their long, athletic legs pushing them quickly away. They disappeared as the curtain of branches closed in after them.

"They're like flying angels of the sacred mountain," Mireya said. She held up Peter's camera. "I think I got our photo of the day."

When we got back to camp, we were shocked to see Mike with blood trickling down his arms, legs, and stomach, as if he'd just stepped out of a crime scene. "They got me!" he shouted. "Those little vampires got me!" It turned out that he'd been feeling better and gone off exploring on his own when the leeches had dropped from the sky like rain.

That night at dinner, we discussed strategy. How would we follow the seven "silkies" in this steep landscape? How would we capture them and get the necessary data? In the old days, primatologists accomplished their science through observations of behavior. But now, with modern technology, observation wasn't enough. We'd have to shoot the animals with the dart gun; put collars on them for radio tracking; and take body measurements, photos, blood samples, and tissue samples for genetic and biomedical analysis. That liquid nitrogen tank hadn't been carried upright to the top of the mountain for nothing.

Our first problem was the dart gun, which, in Loret's words, was *tsimba*, or broken. Thinking it was just rusty, Loret had tried oiling it, but the gun wouldn't shoot. We used Peter's satellite phone, with which he'd been sending the photos for *NOVA*, to call Charlie Welch, who had a dart gun at Parc Ivoloina in Toamasina. Charlie sent the gun to the Ranomafana National Park office in Tana, and Herizo, a graduate student who was working there, boarded the next available flight to Sambava, the closest town with an airport to Marojejy National Park. Then Herzio hired a cab to the base of Mount Marojejy, and the guides met him there and carried the gun up. This only took two days, and fortunately the anesthetic darts from the first gun fit into this second weapon.

The next problem was finding the silkies again. However, this turned out to be much easier. The morning we received the second dart gun, we spotted them in a location close to where we'd first seen them. Loret aimed and fired, and the pink-faced male fell like a piece of fruit from a tree. The other guides caught him in a net and laid him on the ground. We took measurements, dorsal and ventral photographs, and prepared tissue samples to be lowered into the liquid nitrogen tank. Like a surgeon's arena in a hospital, we worked quickly and in near silence. The final step was to weigh each sifaka using a Pesola scale. These sifakas were larger than those I was used to in Ranomafana. The pink-faced male weighed 16.1 pounds, while the largest Milne-Edwards' sifaka had been recorded at 13.9 pounds and most Milne-Edwards' adults at 12.8 pounds. Within three hours we'd finished collecting the first biomedical data ever on the silky sifaka. We released the animals and smiled as they all leaped back to the forest.

That night, we celebrated around the campfire. Peter, whose feet were almost healed, shared his bars of Swiss chocolate. The Malagasies sang and drummed on the cooking pots. Mike began to dance like a wild beast, then dropped to the ground on all fours, dipping his face toward the ground. He jutted his chin toward the sky and sprang on all his limbs to the rhythm of the drumbeat. I wondered if his illness had come back and he'd gone mad.

"He's dancing the crocodile dance!" Mireya laughed. "In Sambava, they dance the crocodile dance to celebrate good things and to ward off evil."

None of us knew where Mike had learned this crocodile dance, but we cheered him on all the same.

Despite the swollen foot, wriggly leeches, fevers, and the broken gun, the expedition was a complete success. Mireya would go on to cowrite a paper, "Specific status of *Propithecus* spp" (*International Journal of Primatology* 25:875–900, 2004), which proved by comparing both nuclear and mitochondrial DNA, *Propithecus diadema candidus*, the silky sifaka, was its very own species. This was the first of many accomplishments that would distinguish her career. Mike Kraus became a physicist. And although Peter Tyson hadn't quite documented his trip for *NOVA* in the way he wished, he ended up writing the critically acclaimed book *The Eighth Continent: Life, Death and Discovery in the Lost World of Madagascar.*

CHAPTER ELEVEN

THE AMANDA TRAIL

(1999–2000)

A S PART OF HER STUDIES at Boston University, Amanda had spent a year studying French in Grenoble and interning for the Ministry of Culture in Paris. When she graduated, her only aspiration was to move to New York City, much to my dismay. She took an entry-level job with Brink's, a security logistics company, in 1997. At twenty-seven, after a hefty bonus from Brink's and with her relationship with her French boyfriend failing, she decided to travel through Europe visiting friends. In early November 1999, I called Amanda to find out her plans for the holidays.

I suggested that she come to Madagascar. "I'm going with an Earthwatch team. We can spend Christmas in Isalo National Park. Then, if you want, you can come with me to spend New Year's in Helsinki with Jukka."

Amanda thought this was an excellent plan. "Mom, you know it is 1999, and with the rumors of technological disaster, I think Madagascar would be a good place to spend the New Year. It won't even be affected by any issues with Y2K."

Amanda was a fairly private person and had never been very forthcoming about her personal life. I suspected that she was looking for a more stable relationship than the one I'd had with her father, and something more constant than what I had with Jukka. Jukka and I had been able to make our transcontinental relationship work so far, but I knew it wasn't for everyone.

This trip would not only be an opportunity for me to catch up with Amanda, but a chance for her to see old friends. It had been a little over two years since she'd last been to Madagascar. Verne Simons, who was a sophomore at Duke, would be there with his mother, Friderun, while Elwyn was hunting subfossils up north. This would be Verne's third visit to Ranomafana—he said watching *Hapalemur simus* was like watching a fossil come alive. Also visiting Madagascar for the first time would be my brother, Chris Chapple. A professor of Asian religions, Chris had been a guest speaker in India during the previous month and planned on stopping in Madagascar on his way back to Los Angeles, where he lived. We arranged for him to be invited by the University of Fianarantsoa to speak about Malagasy religion and its ideas about the natural world.

We'd also have a chance to make new friends among the Earthwatch team members that would be joining us in Ranomafana National Park. Earthwatch was a program where regular people such as schoolteachers, accountants, and architects could volunteer to help not-so-regular people such as field biologists, archeologists, and paleontologists for two weeks on a particular project. Each volunteer paid a bit extra for the experience. This program provided a valuable source of funding for my research (it mostly went to pay the guides' salaries) during gaps between substantial federal grants. Eight Earthwatchers had signed up for this trip: four twenty-year-old women and four men, including a forty-year-old who'd made a fortune in gumball machines, a veterinarian from England, and a schoolteacher from Meaford, Canada, the town in southern Ontario where my father was from. Chris and I would have plenty to talk to him about!

Only days before the trip was about to start, I received news from Blue Magruder, Earthwatch's public relations director, that she was sending along a journalist and a photographer to document the expedition. I met the two of them at the airport in Tana. Steven Kotler, the journalist, was wiry and witty with short hair and dark glasses that looked like goggles. The photographer, Miguel Poston, was tall and lanky with dreadlocks. Both were around thirty years of age.

"I'm from Los Angeles," Steve told me during our drive to Ranomafana. "I'm working on a book about surfing in California."

Steve went on to explain that he'd been commissioned for two articles, one on Ranomafana National Park and the second on Andringitra, which would be a national park soon. Just south of Ranomafana, Andringitra was famous for its high peaks, especially the Tsaranoro Massif. The champion rock climber Lynn Hill had already scaled the peak and her paeans of praise for its vistas had set off a flurry of chatter in the climbing world.

"What about you?" I asked Miguel. "Where are you from?"

"San Francisco," he replied. "I used to be a fashion photographer but got tired of taking pictures of dresses."

I assured Miguel that he'd never get tired of taking pictures of lemurs. The road was long and somewhere toward the end of the trip I learned that both of them had recently become romantically unattached.

By the time we reached Ranomafana it was dark. The next morning, I took the Earthwatch team to see Group I and to start training them on how to take data on the behavior and ecology of sifakas. They were going to pick a focal animal for the day and write down the activities of the lemurs every five minutes. Steven and Miguel shadowed the Earthwatchers, taking notes and photos of them.

Amanda was delighted to be back in the forest. When we got to the cabin, she was disappointed that no one was watching the sifaka groups, as it was trail-upkeep week. She went off on her own to follow the sifakas, and returned beaming from being in the rainforest and proud at having been able to find Group III by herself. The guides walked up the cabin steps where Amanda was staying, laughing rather raucously and mentioning Amanda's name. "What are you talking about?" Amanda aimed her question at Georges in Malagasy.

Georges barked his astonishing, rising laugh, which tended to boom throughout the forest, and I could tell Amanda was noticeably perplexed as the other guides giggled behind him. Georges turned to her: "We were cutting more trails for the Group IV off of T Trail," he said. None of us knew why this was so funny. "We cut one that was very steep to connect from T Trail in the valley to Z Trail. We had used all the letters in the alphabet so we couldn't think about what to name it." Amanda looked dubiously at Georges. "Okay Georges, why is this so funny?" Amanda asked. "We decided to name it the 'Amanda Trail,'" Georges replied with a giggle. "It's the steepest and toughest trail we have ever cut." Amanda smiled and rolled her eyes. We finished lunch and then Amanda took off to take a look at her trail.

Pierre now worked for the park service as a ranger, and Emile and Loret had quarreled with the park staff and decided to work as independent tourist guides. Georges was the head guide for my research team, and he had his own group of younger guides who followed the sifakas.

Amanda had been helping with the Earthwatchers all week and asked for Friday off. She told me in the morning she was just going to walk around the trails and would be back for lunch. Amanda took off and wasn't seen again until dusk.

Amanda knew that Georges was watching Group III. She had wandered down to W Trail, which was her favorite destination when she wanted a bit of peace, since few tourists or even researchers used the path. She ended up wandering back to F Trail and finding Georges. He updated her on Group III and explained that Pale Male was still in the area with his son, Blue Purple. Sadly, when Blue Purple was two years old, his mother and Pale Male's first mate, Judy, had been killed by a fossa. Pale Male himself had almost died from the fossa's teeth as he tried to protect her. Pale Male had left Blue Purple for six months while he'd traveled south to find a new mate, Green

Orange. Now the family lived together with a new baby from Pale Male and Green Orange.

Georges also updated Amanda on his newest wife, and how they'd finally had a son. Amanda was delighted and laughed when she found out he had very traditionally named the boy Georges, after himself. "How about you?" Georges asked in return. "I have no children and I'm still not interested in marriage," Amanda answered. "I have a boyfriend in New York but it isn't working out."

"Why don't you take some data, Amanda?" Georges asked.

"No, I'm not interested. I'm just relaxing in the forest today. I can be your guide if you like?" Amanda teased.

"I don't need a guide," Georges said, "and neither do you, but we do need to take data for Pat."

"No, I have the day off, and besides I don't have any lunch or even water."

"I can share my lunch and water. You can watch Pale Male; I am watching mother Green Orange." Amanda looked over at Georges and he smiled.

"Fine," she said and took out her notebook.

They caught up with their lives, chatting about nothing and everything, laughing occasionally and sitting in comfortable silence—all the while taking data. Amanda had chosen to watch Pale Male, I think, because he was her favorite animal. Although he joined other groups, he always came back to his home group, Group III. She secretly told me "off the records," because she had no scientific evidence, that she thought he was too sweet. He could never bring himself to commit infanticide or fight another male to get accepted into a new group.

Toward the end of the day, Amanda and Georges were getting tired and hungry. The animals were slowly going to their sleep site along the river on FF Trail. They moved quite close to the ground because it was a very steep trail. Amanda was used to the animals being low on this trail and it was not uncommon for them to jump within a meter of you. Amanda was taking a five-minute sample when Pale Male landed about a meter from her. She looked over at him and smiled, standing very still and taking in his beauty, expecting that he'd hop across to the trees on the other side of the trail to where the group's sleep tree was located.

Instead, he looked at her, moved his head back and forth slightly, made an *mmmm* sound at her, and then jumped to a small tree about a foot from where she was standing. Amanda later recounted, "I was so amazed, I couldn't allow myself to breathe. I was scared and delighted at the same time. I just stood as still as I could and then he turned over, showing me his cream-colored belly. He reached out to eat two young leaves that were just burgeoning from a branch. His large canines looked really huge at this distance and, although I knew he wouldn't bite me, I knew that he could.

"His musty lemur smell infused my lungs, and as we looked at each other, he chomped away at the young leaves quite matter-of-factly, while I stared into his beautiful auburn eyes, with my heart racing so fast I thought I'd have a heart attack. I've never been that close to a sifaka for such an extended period of time. It was the most amazing experience. It was like time stood still. It couldn't have been more than a minute out of my life but it felt like an eternity."

Georges had come up behind her, not realizing how close Pale Male was to her. He told her he'd never seen Pale Male that near to anyone before.

"Oh my God, Georges! That was amazing!" Amanda exclaimed. "Thank you so much for making me stay out today!"

"Yes, you had good luck, Amanda," he said. "I am tired. It's Friday, I am going home to my family." He closed his notebook and shook her hand. "Let me know the position of the sleep site and who slept with whom. Next week, I will write it in my book."

"What!" Amanda was aghast. "You can't leave now. They are almost at the sleep site. It isn't fair to leave me out here when I'm not supposed to even be out here."

"I have a family, Amanda," said Georges firmly. "You'll be okay. You don't even need to cook your own dinner." He smiled. "They will be asleep in another thirty minutes. It is good to see you, Amanda. It has been a long time." And with that he vanished down the trail.

"*Veloma*, Georges," Amanda called after him. "I will remember this!"

I tell this story because this would be the last season that Amanda would spend with Pale Male and Georges. They both passed away during the years she wasn't able to come to Madagascar. She recounted this story to me in a moment of reflection about Georges, when she returned to Madagascar years later. She told me she was happy to have had a few moments alone with the animals and take in the experience she'd had with Pale Male, amazed at the fact that she could have just as easily decided not to stay with Georges and take data.

"Life's most precious moments can be determined by a whim," she added. "Isn't that mad, Mom?" She was pleased to have had this day with Georges, because although she'd spend many hours with him afterward, this would be the last day she remembered spending with him. A beautiful memory; an eternal day.

During the first week, the members of the Earthwatch team steadily got the hang of following the sifakas and taking data on them while Steven interviewed them and Miguel took pictures. Ever inquisitive, Steven also interviewed my brother Chris on his thoughts about religion. Chris reflected on his perception, informed by Yoga and meditation, that the world radiates a wholeness, a wisdom without walls, based on interconnection. This rainforest reinforced his perception.

Within a week, using the observational skills I'd honed over the years, I knew my daughter was making an impression. Steven would tell me how smart and well-read my daughter was. "She knows T. S. Eliot's poems and can recite passages from *Don Quixote*," he marveled. "I start reciting a poem and she finishes it. You're so lucky to have such an intellectual daughter." Then Miguel would come and tell me how quickly Amanda moved through the forest and how keenly she observed the animals. "My father was a veterinarian in San Francisco," he said. "We always had a menagerie of animals at home." But I received no clues from Amanda about her feelings. I tried to judge how Amanda felt about the journalist and the photographer. There had to be clues as to which one she liked better. But Amanda was kind and gracious to everyone.

Two weeks goes quickly and our time with the Earthwatch team rapidly drew to a close. Steven told me that he and Miguel needed a guide who spoke both French and Malagasy for their work in Andringitra, and could Amanda come with them? I gave my permission. The three of them went off to the south, and I finished up with the Earthwatchers, who'd learned much about the life of sifakas, and I'd gained two weeks of "field follow" data. They were intrigued with the soap-opera lives of the sifakas. During the second week of December, I noticed that the adult male in Group II moved sweetly up to the female and gave a soft "love call" and kissed her mouth to mouth. Then he deftly mounted her for thirty seconds and afterward they groomed for ten minutes. The Earthwatchers jumped with joy to see a mating. I explained how lucky they were. Female sifakas are in estrus, and encourage mating, only twenty-four hours in a year. *Twenty-four hours!* These two mated twice more before the sun went down. What a wonderful way to end an Earthwatch adventure! Just before dark, my brother Chris and I walked in the forest and saw two red-tailed vanga chicks venture from the edge of their nest—probably their first flight. "What a beautiful rainforest this is," said Chris. At our farewell party that night, the group danced almost to dawn.

Amanda came back to Ranomafana alone, once Steven and Miguel had left for the States. I was dying to know what had gone on during their trip, but she said nothing. Christmas was only a few days away, so Amanda, my Stony Brook graduate student Sarah Karpanty, and an Earthwatcher named Jax, who'd decided to stay behind, and I started our ten-hour drive to Isalo National Park. Located in the southwest near the town of Ihosy, Isalo is best known for its sandstone massif. Eighty miles long and about thirty miles wide, it is called the Grand Canyon of Madagascar. At a distance, it looks like a layer cake of muted pink and brown, with a splattering of Day-Glo colors produced by red, black, and lime-green lichen.

On Christmas Eve, Amanda, Sarah, Jax, and I hiked through the forested canyons within the sandstone mountain range, where we saw ring-tailed lemurs, white sifakas, and brown lemurs feeding in the trees along the streams. We stopped at Namaza Falls, the most spectacular waterfall in Isalo, which plunges one hundred and fifty feet into a pool ringed by green cascades of ferns. Blue-winged Malachite kingfishers perched on flowered branches and darted over the pool to catch insects.

That night, we retired to the Relais de la Reine Hotel, owned by a hospitable French family, for a delicious seven-course meal laced with glasses of wine. We swapped stories from the field and laughed, especially at Sarah's tales of her bird studies. For her dissertation project, Sarah was looking at seven species of raptors in Ranomafana to see if any of them preyed on lemurs, something no one had ever done before. When she suggested this topic, I was convinced that only the tiny mouse lemurs fell prey to hawks and eagles. I challenged Sarah to prove me wrong.

Sarah had begun her research funded by two back-to-back Earthwatch groups. One of these Earthwatchers was Charlie

Wexler, a keen birder and founder of the World Resources Institute, a global research organization that addressed environmental and conservation issues. Charlie wanted to see the nest of a Henst's goshawk, which had a wingspan of three feet and talons and beaks evolved for killing.

"The chicks, just two white balls of fluff, were crouched in their nest a hundred feet high," Sarah related. "Charlie put a comfortable chair underneath it and settled there with a cold drink and his binoculars. But the raptor parents got suspicious and decided to watch *him*. They spent the entire morning perched above him staring at his broad-brimmed hat. The chicks remained hungry until Charlie went to lunch."

Sarah watched the goshawk nest the following day. She didn't wear a hat and the birds were used to her. By 8 A.M. the female had carried a dead *Hapalemur griseus* in her talons to feed the two chicks. The small bamboo lemur looked like it weighed just under two pounds.

"Charlie was excited by the news," Sarah continued. "He volunteered to observe the nest the following day. Once again, the two adult birds just stared at him all day long."

The next day at 7 A.M., Sarah observed the male goshawk bring the head of a male brown lemur to the chicks. Loret, who was working with her, had seen the goshawk attack the lemur in the trees, bring it to the ground, divide the corpse with its beak, and fly off with the head in his talons. Over the next month, Sarah saw the hawks eating a diversity of mouse lemurs, dwarf lemurs, and woolly lemurs. I apologized to Sarah for being wrong about the impact of raptor predation on lemur populations.

"What about Charlie?" Amanda asked. "Did he ever get to see the adult hawks bring anything to the chicks?"

"He finally saw a chameleon delivered to the nest." Sarah laughed.

We poured some more red wine and started on another course. I was hoping that Amanda might talk about her trip to Andringitra, but Sarah was starting on another story. She'd observed that the harrier hawk also preyed on lemurs. Sarah and Loret had located seven nests, most on the edge of the park. One particular nest was perched very close to the rice paddies of Ambatovory, outside the park. We'd worked with that village since Lon Kightlinger had set up a health clinic there years previously. Ambatovory had produced great musicians, like Dada Lira who played the *valiha*, a Malagasy zither made out of bamboo. He had sung at the inauguration of the park.

"I explained to the king of the village that I was studying a harrier hawk nest in the area and asked him to please, please not cut down the trees," Sarah said. "When I came back a month later, many of the fields had been slashed and burned and were still smoking. But the king had left the one tree with the nest standing, with the stressed-out bird in it."

"What did you do?" Amanda asked.

"I burst into tears. The king thought he'd saved my tree and was totally confused. I explained that I had meant he shouldn't cut down all the trees in the area in order to protect the bird."

"Communication is the key to conservation," I pointed out. "Sometimes, even when both sides act in good faith, it doesn't quite work out."

Sarah nodded. "But there's a happy ending."

Ambatovory's king was very old, and he became sick. He called all his relatives together and recounted the promise he'd given Sarah a year before. The king explained that in honor of the harrier hawk, and in honor of Sarah, all of his lands would go back to the forest. Most of his sons had gone to work in the town of Ranomafana. He wanted them to return to Ambatovory and plant trees in all his fields close to the park.

"I was amazed and touched," Sarah said. "Nobody will go against the king's last wishes, so that land is going to be reforested and protected from now on. I guess sometimes conservation can work in surprising ways."

The three of us toasted the memory of the King of Ambatovory with our dessert of chocolate mousse and a glass of cognac.

On Christmas Day, our driver, Dede, suggested we go visit Ilakaka, a town only fifteen minutes from our hotel. I'd been there seven years before with Peter Reinthal, the fish biologist, when we searched in the Ilakaka River for the trondo mainty, *Ptychochromoides besileanus*, a rare species of fish with a bump on its forehead. At the time, the town consisted of three thatched-roof adobe huts, and we asked the children from those huts to help us catch the fish. As the story goes, in 1998 one of those boys from Ilakaka found a sapphire worth thousands of United States dollars in the bank of the river and sold it to a Thai gem dealer for the equivalent of one or two dollars. Within a few months, gem traders from other parts of Africa, Thailand, and Sri Lanka flooded the area and turned it into a "sapphire rush" town.

By the time we arrived in Ilakaka a year after the sapphire's discovery, the population had grown from twelve to three thousand and the place was a shantytown of makeshift dwellings, casinos, car dealers, and bordellos. From a distance, it looked and smelled like a huge city dump. Piles of sand dotted the banks of the river like huge anthills where miners desperately searched for precious stones. The Ilakaka River was filled with people swishing pebbles in homemade strainers. After finding a few high-quality sapphires, a farmer who previously owned an oxcart could buy a new four-wheel vehicle. And of course, with this newfound wealth came lawlessness. It was said that a murder occurred in Ilakaka every day. Dede cautioned us to keep our windows rolled up, and I, for one, was glad to leave the town.

We started our journey back to Ranomafana National Park to let Sarah off. Amanda, Jax, and I would continue to Tana. All this time, Amanda had not mentioned either the journalist or the photographer. I thought to myself that maybe I'd been wrong about a romance with one of them. But I didn't dare broach the subject.

Within a few days of the heat, desperation, and squalor of Ilakaka, Amanda and I found ourselves in Helsinki, where a foot of snow covered the ground. On New Year's Eve, Jukka, Amanda, and I walked downtown to see the fireworks light up the city. Back at our apartment, Amanda went to sleep on the couch. At 3:45 A.M. the phone rang, waking all of us up. Jukka answered it.

"You want to speak to Amanda?" he asked. "It's three in the morning here. Call her back later." And he slammed down the phone.

"Who is it?" I wanted to know.

"He didn't identify himself," Jukka said.

I looked at Amanda, but she just smiled. Was it the journalist or the photographer?

The following week, when we were back in the United States, Amanda told me that she was moving to San Francisco to spend time with Miguel, the photographer.

me that when he was looking at satellite images of Madagas-

CHAPTER TWELVE

THE CREATURE OF KALAMBATRITRA

(2000)

L OCATED IN southeastern Madagascar, about seventy miles from the town of Ihosy, Kalambatritra Reserve is so remote that it takes more than two days to drive to the end of the closest road and then another two days to trek east to the forest. Glen Green, a remote-sensing specialist, told me that when he was looking at satellite images of Madagascar in 1990, Kalambatritra looked like the ideal place to find the extinct subfossil lemurs alive. The forested area was large enough to hold a relict population, but isolated enough that people wouldn't have passed through. So far, five biologists had visited Kalambatritra, and they'd only spent half a day there before returning to the nearby town of Betroka. The only lemur ever seen in this reserve had been identified as a "brown lemur." Among researchers, Kalambatritra was known as the last unexplored rainforest in Madagascar. I hoped it contained not only the brown lemur, but other, more unusual animals who might reveal themselves to us.

Ever since, years ago, I'd heard about the mysterious creature,

"something big" near the village of Amparafitra, I'd wanted
to go look for it in Kalambatritra Reserve, which was directly
south. I didn't have the chance, though, until I put together a
team for a biodiversity survey there. Although our main goal
would be the survey, we also planned to investigate by the
Ianaivo River, which originated in Amparafitra, and where I
thought "something big" might be. Jukka begged off this trip.
Perhaps the memories of the last expedition were too fresh in
his mind. Mitch Irwin, my Canadian graduate student, and his
fiancée Karen Samonds agreed to lead the lemur team. Karen
had studied paleontology with Professor David Krause at Stony
Brook University, and she had previously looked for dinosaur
bones in northwestern Madagascar. Loret would be in charge
of the team that listed birds; Jean Luc Raharison, a University
of Antananarivo graduate student, would assist with the primate surveys; and an ecologist named Pascal Rabeson would
head the botany and stream insect team.

As usual, the trip started off with unforeseen problems when
we ran out of gas halfway to Betroka. We slept in the vehicle
and in the morning a kind truck driver gave us enough fuel to
make it the rest of the way. Once in town, as usual, we located
the mayor's office to get our permits approved. But when we
showed the mayor our authorization for a biodiversity study in
Kalambatritra Reserve, he shook his head.

"It's too dangerous right now," he said. "*Qat*, a special kind
of hashish, is being grown west of the reserve. The *dahalos*,
the cattle rustlers, take it north to the market, armed with
guns. I think you should do this expedition later, next year or
the year after."

This was a big setback. I had never even heard of there being a narcotics industry, or any drug problems, in Madagascar.

Then Pascal spoke. "Would it be possible for you to send armed guards with us? We would pay." He looked at me and added, "We would pay double."

The mayor agreed. The next day, with porters and two soldier escorts, our research team began our two-day walk to the edge of the reserve. Located in southeastern Madagascar, this rainforest lay between the Ianaivo River catchment area to the east and Ihosy River basin to the west. The summit of the highest peak topped out at almost 6,000 feet.

In two days, we only passed one village. The local people, the Bara, were known for their vast numbers of cattle. Indeed, a man's wealth was measured by how many zebu he owned. Young Bara men were not allowed to marry until they'd rustled enough cattle to show that they had the means to protect and care for a wife. Sometimes a man had more than one wife, and thus more cattle were required. The Bara lived on the grassland with their zebu and rarely entered the forest. When we looked for a place to set up our camp, we saw very little evidence of human disturbance.

The first day, we came across what we assumed was a group of seventeen brown lemurs. Marian Nicoll, a botanist from the United Kingdom, was the first to observe a brown lemur in Kalambatritra in 1989, and had identified these animals as possibly being red-fronted brown lemurs, a species also found in Ranomafana. Curious, the group came close and peered down at us with their deep amber eyes, making little pig-like grunts, the signature sound for brown lemurs. These lemurs had jet-black faces and tails to match, as well as plush russet-red bodies. But their distinguishing characteristic was their bright orange, bushy beards. It turned out that what we were looking at were not red-fronted brown lemurs at all, but rather the collared lemur (*Eulemur collaris*). This kind of lemur had been determined to be a separate species from the brown lemur by Professor Yves Rumpler and individuals had been spotted further southeast in Midongy du Sud National Park. We could now confirm with photos that *Eulemur collaris* had also been found in Kalambatritra Reserve.

Buoyed by this discovery, we continued to cut a mile-and-a-quarter trail for the biodiversity surveys. The trees were taller than any I'd seen before in Madagascar, rising 130 feet into the air, and the trunks were three feet in girth. Many of them were typical Malagasy hardwoods, including rosewood, but no logging was permitted here. Also forbidden was the cutting of *Pandanus* leaves to make mats or smoking out trees to get honey. Instead of cut marks on their bark, the trees were dripping with moss and orchids.

In addition to the collared lemur, we sighted the eastern lesser bamboo lemur, a pair of adults with one subadult and a yearling. The adults were much larger than those in Ranomafana. However, we didn't glimpse the other two species of bamboo lemurs—the golden bamboo lemur and the greater bamboo lemur. We also didn't observe black-and-white ruffed lemurs or sifakas, as there were in Ranomafana. The nocturnal surveys were more fruitful. The first night we saw two sportive lemurs and mouse lemurs high in the trees. The most exciting find was the teeth gauges of an aye-aye in a dead log, perhaps toppled by a cyclone. Since there were many of these marks, we suspected a high population of aye-ayes in this area.

We were into our second week of the lemur surveys when Loret arrived back at camp, breathless. "Red owl. . . . I've seen the red owl," he managed to say.

The red owl was one of the rarest raptors in Madagascar. As far as we knew, it didn't eat lemurs, feeding instead on insects and frogs. It had only previously been seen up north, in Andasibe.

"Mitch!" I shouted. "Get your camera. We need to take a photo!"

Mitch and I plunged after Loret into the forest. And indeed, we noticed an owl the size of a fist and with reddish, black-spotted plumage, sleeping in the palm leaves. It stirred and blinked at the flash of the camera.

"Loret, you've just extended the geographic range of this rare bird over five hundred miles," I said. "This is very good news, indeed."

The lemur surveys continued slowly until one night when Mitch saw not eyeshine, but another indication that there might be a lemur around: a pile of dung. A big pile of dung, actually; eighteen inches wide, one foot long, and two inches deep. What could be doing this? Lemurs had never been observed to have regular places where they deposited feces. Could whatever was doing this be a carnivore of some type? With a leaf, Mitch picked up one of the green pellets and took a sniff—it was not odiferous enough to have come from a fossa. He began to count the pellets one by one and reached 192. How many animals had used this spot? And for how many days? At 6:30 P.M. Mitch replaced the dung and covered the pile with leaves to see if the animal would return to make another deposit.

Back at camp, Mitch told us his dung story. No one had ever heard of dung piles on the ground in the rainforest. We'd read about fat-tailed dwarf lemurs smearing their nests with feces to mark their territory, but this was different. Then I remembered the study I conducted in Anamalazoatra Reserve near Périnet in the east. For four months, I'd followed a family of eastern lesser bamboo lemurs from dawn to dusk and observed that they seemed to defecate in one place. First, the adult female would move down to a vine, lift her tail, make her deposit, and leap away. The subadult female would go next, and the father and baby would follow suit. This behavior happened throughout the course of my bamboo lemur study. I'd wondered about this habit, but had never had a chance to follow up on it. Maybe Mitch's mysterious depositor was a bamboo lemur.

The next morning at 8:15 Mitch returned to his special bank to see if there were any new deposits.

"Fifteen!" he reported when he came back to camp. "Fifteen new pieces on the pile. And these pieces are huge. There's no way this creature can be a lemur."

"These pieces are bigger than sifaka feces, and my sifaka weigh thirteen pounds," I observed. "They deposit a maximum of four or five fecal pellets at a time. In fact, they only defecate about three times a day. Your animal is, well . . ."

"Very productive," Mitch supplied.

"You'd better keep a careful track of this pile. This could be a new species. What should we call it? Not 'big foot.'"

Mitch ignored the bad joke. "The pile is under a Dombeya." Dombeyas were fast-growing trees that shot up after periods of great rain, such as a cyclone. "The tree has gashes on the trunk, about half-an-inch long and very thin. They're single gashes, not double as they would be if they were made by canines."

"Like a gash made from a spur? Bamboo lemurs have spurs on their wrists, made from material like human fingernails. Could it be that?"

Mitch invited everyone to come take a look, which we did at 10 A.M. No one had any insights, so Mitch covered the pile with leaves and we all left the scene. Between 10:55 P.M. and 5:15 A.M. an additional twelve deposits were made. Obviously, a stakeout was in order.

In the meantime, the soldier escorts the mayor had sent with us were becoming nervous. Pascal told us that they missed their families and wanted to return to Betroka. Also, they were asking what we were really doing in the forest. They were afraid that there were "little people with their feet on backwards" among the trees.

"That's it," I said to Mitch. "These little people with their feet on backwards are using your latrine."

Mitch was very serious about the stakeout. He built a small makeshift hut out of sticks and palm fronds that could fit one person. A tiny window was left open, big enough for the camera. The first day went by and no new pellets were added to the pile. Then Mitch came rushing back to camp at 8:30 P.M., extremely flustered.

"I fell asleep, for only about fifteen minutes. When I woke

up there were fourteen pieces on the pile. I can't believe I fell asleep and missed it!"

At least he'd learned that the animal was nocturnal. And that the creature of the latrine couldn't be a eastern lesser bamboo lemur, because they were active during the daylight hours.

The rest of the team continued with nocturnal censuses. For each census, the following information was recorded: date, time, trail, census team, and weather. In addition, for each lemur sighting, the following information was recorded: time, position on trail, species/subspecies, age and sex of each individual seen, sighting distance, sighting angle (relative to trail), perpendicular distance (distance from trail), height, group spread, activity, who detected the animals, method of detection, and miscellaneous observations. Night after night, we walked the trail searching for lemurs, until seventeen censuses were completed.

Then one day, Mitch announced he'd found another "special pile" about half a mile from the first. It was next to a tree trunk that had the signature scratch marks. Mitch was convinced that scratching was a common behavior to this big creature. Two days later, he found a third pile, only a quarter of a mile from the first. Mitch continued his nocturnal vigils at the first pile, going to the blind each night, but the giant defecator continued to elude him.

Finally, one night Mitch saw an animal in the trees. He readied the camera as the creature descended to a branch just over the pile. The flash went off and the animal jumped back, disappearing into the foliage. Mitch had captured the creature on film, but he still didn't know what it was.

The following night he didn't take the camera, just a flashlight with a red plastic lens over the light so as not to upset the animal. Around midnight, the creature descended to a branch over the pile. This time, Mitch saw it clearly. It was a sportive lemur—a big-bodied sportive lemur with a gray head, large ears, a russet-colored back, beige underparts, and a dark tail. It tipped its body forward, lifted its tail, and made a distinct deposit. And then another one. The mystery was solved. This was indeed a lemur latrine. But this sportive lemur looked to be twice the size of other sportive lemurs. Could it be a new species? Mitch rushed back to camp to share the good news.

The next morning of the census transect Mitch found two of these large sportive lemurs in a sleeping hole thirteen feet high in a large Tambourissa tree. Mitch took clear and definitive photos. He suspected that the two adults were a pair and wondered if this was mating season. Further observation showed that these sportive lemurs' territorial calls were raucous and lively. The males had redder heads and the females' head color was grayer. If this sexual dimorphism held, meaning that the male and female had different phenotypic characteristics, this would be the first sexually dichromatic *Lepilemur* species.

Lepilemurs, or sportive lemurs, had been placed in the Megaladapidae family along with the large chimpanzee-sized subfossils, *Megaladapis edwardsi* and *Megaladapis madagascariensis*, but later genetic evidence disproved this relationship. Although they are called "sportive" because they use their fists when captured, a more appropriate name might be "leaping lemurs," as they have long hind legs that propel them merrily through the forest.

There are more than nine species of *Lepilemur* distinguished by genetic analysis. These lemurs eat a monotonous diet of leaves, leaves, and leaves. Dr. Jörg Ganzhorn from Hamburg University performed a chemical analysis of the leaves eaten by *Lepilemur* that revealed they can eat leaves full of alkaloids, the same compound found in strychnine, nicotine, quinine, and cocaine. Perhaps it is coincidental, but *Lepilemurs* are also distinguished by having the smallest brain size for their body weight of any lemur. The white-footed sportive lemur (*Lepilemur leucopus*), the species found nearest to Kalambatritra, weighs ten ounces and has white feet. Dr. Leanne Nash from Arizona State University wrote a paper on them called "Vertical Clingers and Sleepers: Seasonal Influences on the Activities and Substrate Use of *Lepilemur leucopus* at Beza Mahafaly Special Reserve" (*Folia Primatologica* 69, Suppl 1. 204–17). The punchline was that this species had low energetic output.

By the time we'd completed our survey, we'd found more than four hundred species of plants, many of them new to science; a high diversity of insects, reptiles, and amphibians; and fifty-two species of birds, from the red-headed Madagascar flufftail to the white-plumaged crested ibis. We'd also discovered two species of diurnal and five species of nocturnal lemurs. We'd hoped to see aye-ayes, but all we encountered were the traces of tooth gnaws on numerous dead tree trunks. Overall, the primate population density and species richness, especially for the day-active species, appeared to be lower in Kalambatritra than in Ranomafana.

Now that we'd finished at this campsite, we decided to move our tents east toward the Ianaivo River to look for some swamp creatures. My hidden agenda, of course, was to search for "something big." But our soldier escorts were getting edgy, and they insisted that we leave for Betroka. So we packed up the tents and equipment and began to trek west. Our expedition was over for this time. We'd found one new species, the big sportive lemur with the peculiar toilet habits. It wasn't the "something big" that I'd hoped for—indeed, I would never find the mysterious "something big" or the Rano-omby-be—but this was large enough. We published our paper: Irwin MT, Samonds KE, Raharison JL, Wright PC. 2004. "Lemur Latrines: Observations of Latrine Behavior in Wild Primates and Possible Ecological Significance," *Journal of Mammalogy* 85:420–27.

It wasn't until the next year that a team headed by Dr. Ed Louis, Director of Conservation Genetics at Omaha's Henry Doorly Zoo, returned to Kalambatritra to capture the big sportive lemur. After another few years in the laboratory during which its DNA was studied, this lemur was indeed declared a new species. Ed Louis named it *Lepilemur wrightae*, Wright's sportive lemur.

Lepilemur wrightae, which marked its territory with piles of dung, was larger than the other species of that genus. We also found the males had more of a reddish tone on their backs, another characteristic not found in this very gray group of lemurs. Having a species named after me was a unique privilege. Hundreds of years from now, long after I was gone, "my" lemur would remind people that I had once loved the island called Madagascar.

CHAPTER THIRTEEN

LORET'S LAND

(2001–03)

I N MORE THAN ten years since its inception, Rano-mafana National Park had grown from a wilderness with few amenities to a place where researchers came to study animals and plants, and tourists to witness Madagascar's bounty in a safe and ecological manner. However, although the park contained a primitive research cabin, similar to Cocha Cashu in Peru's Manú National Park, where I'd studied owl monkeys in the early 1980s, it wasn't enough to fit our needs. Biologists observing fish, butterflies, spiders, chameleons, frogs, birds, orchids, and lemurs needed a place to keep their equipment dry and to eat dinner. I had wanted to build a research station inside the park, next to a waterfall, but the park director cautioned me. Anything that was inside the park belonged to the state, and the National Science Foundation refused to give us funding if we didn't officially own the land. So, Loret offered to sell me his land, seven acres next to the main road overlooking the Namorona River and outside the park.

Loret had inherited this land from his family, but selling it to me wasn't so simple. The World Bank had recently come to town with a project that encouraged local residents to measure their land and purchase a proper deed for it. The rationale was that people who officially owned land would farm it sustainably rather than using slash-and-burn techniques. Loret paid for the surveyers and paperwork to obtain the deed from his salary as a guide, and the land was legally owned by him. All I had to do was pay Loret and the deed would be transferred to me. Then we could break ground on the research station.

Of course, bureaucracy is never simple, and that was the case in Madagascar, especially when it came to land. After I thought the transaction had been completed, Loret came to me, apologetic.

"I'm sorry, Madame Patricia," he said, "but my family says I can't sell the land to you."

"Why not?" I was genuinely puzzled.

"They are saying that my great-grandfather, now dead, gave the land to all fifteen members in the family. They are saying that I don't have the right to sell it."

"Let me talk to them," I pleaded. It took some persuading, but eventually Loret said he would gather the members of his family together one afternoon at our research station inside the park and let me speak before them. It was a considerable gathering of Loret's parents, grandparents, brothers and sisters, and their offspring.

We sat on benches at the research station. I started by saying how valued Loret was to me and the other researchers at Ranomafana. Over the past fifteen years, he had been with me—from the discovery of the golden bamboo lemur to the silky sifaka. Loret had sharp eyes that could identify birds quickly, and we had been on most expeditions together. Being a guide paid well, and Loret had found a wife and raised several children with his salary. But these arguments didn't sway his family. Each member in turn rose to tell me why Loret was wrong and how he didn't have exclusive rights to that land. Finally, I stood up to begin my *kabary*, or discourse, holding Loret's deed in my hand. (In Malagasy culture, only the oldest and wisest could give the *kabary*: the longer the oration, the more prestigious the person.)

"I understand that there is a problem. This paper from the government of Madagascar, this deed, states that it is Loret who is the owner of this land. I have paid him for this land and now, according to the government of Madagascar, I own it." I could feel the family members begin to grumble, but I continued.

"I also know that we are one family. We researchers have worked together with you for fifteen years, side by side in the forest with so many of your children and grandchildren. I know that when your ancestor gave you the land years ago, he meant all of you, not just Loret. I am very sad to have caused such strife in the family. But this is the law of the government." One of the elders jumped up with a scowl on his face, and I rushed on.

"I will honor the ancestor's law, too. I will pay exactly the same price that I paid to Loret to the family. I will pay for the land twice."

The family rose and cheered, and Loret smiled. This was a

tremendous amount of money for them. I began to count out the bills as they each signed the deed. The total was 16 million Malagasy ariary or $8,000. The sum would allow each member of the family to buy two zebu or send all their children to school that year. Finally, we were able to start to build.

Finding money to construct the research station was not easy, as funding agencies generally don't want to invest in "bricks and mortar." But I did obtain a National Science Foundation "facilities upgrade grant" of $250,000. Stony Brook University matched that amount. I found a wonderful architect named Peter Ozolins who'd worked in Madagascar for the Lutheran Church building churches, schools, and hospitals, and thus understood the challenges of the island. Loret's plot of land was small, steep, and overrun with streams. The building would be eight thousand square feet and three stories high, with balconies that touched the forest canopy. The bottom floor would hold a conference room, the middle story would provide workspace for the researchers, and the top would house the dining room. There would be hot showers and flush toilets, but the researchers would still live in tents. The money I obtained was enough to build one floor, which was finished in 2001. Where to get the rest?

Funding from outside the United States was a possibility. I'd presented several talks on my research to the biology department at the University of Helsinki, where Jukka taught, and the university had made me a research associate. Together, Jukka and I were studying the patterns of tooth wear in sifakas. I had hoped to encourage more scientists from Finland to come to Madagascar, and it seemed my plan was working. Jukka

Lehtonen had begun studying the effects of invasive rodents on the populations of native rodents, and Jari Niemelä and his graduate students were examining the speciation and ecology of beetles. Then, Jari became a dean at the university. On one of my trips to Helsinki I explained to him my problems with funding the new research station, and within a few days we were in university president Kari Raivio's office with the architect's blueprints. We walked out of the office with a promise of an additional $250,000, which the National Science Foundation matched. That got us to the second floor, but it still wasn't enough.

The final amount came from an unlikely place. At the time, we were negotiating with UNESCO for them to consider Ranomafana National Park among a cluster of other parts of the rainforest as a World Heritage Site. UNESCO told us we needed to upgrade our facilities before we'd be considered "worthy" of the approval. We needed to improve the paths within the park for tourists, build bridges over the rivers for better access, and upgrade the research facilities. We received about $80,000 to finish the research station from UNESCO.

Next, the research station needed to be staffed. I hired a French botanist, Jean Philippe Puyravaud, to be its first director. The other staff members would be Malagasy who'd worked with us for years and knew Ranomafana well. Jean Claude Razafimahaimodison, Steve Zack's student who had earned a PhD from the University of Massachusetts, Amherst, on the effects of tourism on birds in Ranomafana National Park, returned from the United States to become the head of research. Florent Ravoavy, a dinosaur biologist and former director of the Ranomafana Park Museum, became head of the health, education, and reforestation team. As our department head for partnerships, we chose Pascal Rabeson. He'd begun his career fishing with Peter Reinthal and then became an ant expert with Gary Alpert of Harvard University. He'd earned a masters degree from the University of Georgia Institute of Ecology, and had worked as an expedition coordinator for Brian Fisher from the California Academy of Sciences.

To round out the team I needed a head of logistics and audiovisual communication. The first person who came to mind was Dede Randrianarisata, the former driver, who'd taken courses at Stony Brook University in video and editing. Loret Rasabo and Emile Rajerarison wanted to continue as specialist tourist guides, but promised to assist us in teaching classes and with film crews when we needed them. Georges Rakotonirina became the head of the lemur guides.

Finally, we needed a name for the research station. For that, I consulted Benjamin Andriamihaja, who ran the Ranomafana office in Tana. "The Ranomafana National Park Research Station" was my original suggestion.

"This station is more than Ranomafana," Benjamin pointed out. "It will be the hub of research for the whole region." He paused. "How about Centre de Valorization de la Biodiversité?"

"'The Center for the Valuing of Biodiversity,'" I repeated. "Yes, that captures the spirit of the place—understanding and conserving the rainforest to make the region better for both the wildlife and the people. But the name is too long."

"Call it Centre ValBio," Benjamin suggested.

Centre ValBio it was. Back at Stony Brook, Milton Glaser,

the artist who designed the "I [Heart] NY" logo, worked his wonders for Centre ValBio for free. In the middle of the logo is the face of a lemur:

In June 2003, we inaugurated the center. The President of the University of Helsinki, Kari Raivio, and Jari Niemelä joined Jukka as the Finnish delegation. The architect Peter Ozolins, my brother Ted, and Dave Haring from Duke University arrived to help celebrate. The roof of the building wasn't quite finished, but the balconies touched the canopy of trees as I took Dave and Ted on a tour. "As if treating the station as part of the landscape," I told them, "mouse lemurs came into the kitchen for bananas last night. You can see wagtails and drongo birds perched on the balcony railings to catch insects in the morning. Look up there! It's a Henst's goshawk atop the roof. Yesterday, we saw brown lemurs leaping in the nearby trees, and we could almost touch them from this balcony." Three stories below, the Namorona River rushed past in a perpetual, soothing hum.

At about 7 A.M. the traditional killing of the zebu took place. These zebu had been staked out in the grassy "lawn" next to the building near the Namorona River. Four kings from four villages near the edge of the park, with their ceremonial *lambdas* slung over their shoulders, stood facing east and began the incantation for the ancestors. After they told the ancestors that a zebu was being killed in their honor, and offered them a libation, four strong, courageous young men stepped forth to wrestle with the zebu. According to tradition, they would pin it to the ground, tie the back legs of the animal, and then cut its throat. I loved animals and I had trouble watching an animal being slaughtered.

At noon, the speeches began in the outdoor pavilion on the east side of Centre ValBio. More than a thousand people were in attendance, Malagasy and western dignitaries alike. Many of the Malagasies wore traditional four-cornered raffia hats. Women in long green gowns, their hair wreathed in flowers, lined the descending granite staircase. After thanking the research team, the architects, and the donors for making this research station possible, the Minister of Environment turned to me. He pinned a Medal of Honor on my shoulder— my second. My first medal, the Chevalier (Knighthood) had been awarded to me in 1995 in honor of my work creating the Ranomafana National Park. My heart swelled as I accepted this second medal from Madagascar and listened to the Minister's words: "With great pride, we acknowledge your incredible work for the betterment of Madagascar." Tears came to my eyes, and I remembered how pleased I'd been at the inauguraton of the park. I felt in my heart how much the lemurs needed saving and how our team had worked so hard. But there was much to do in the future. This medal meant accomplishment and an urgency to do more.

That night, the research station was transformed. Small tables covered with white tablecloths and fresh-cut flowers dotted its outside surroundings. Dinner of rice and zebu meat was served from our new kitchen. The outdoor classroom housed the local band and the loudspeakers, as well as a wooden dance floor that rocked with revelers. Drinks were served out of the storage shed. The evening was magical.

"I didn't think this building would ever be finished," I said to Guy Suzon, Director of the National Park Service.

"Patricia, this building is an honor for Madagascar. You deserve that medal on your shoulder. And what a wonderful party! Shall we dance?" And off we went to the floor.

The one person I wished could have been at the inauguration was Amanda. Following her move to San Francisco, she and Miguel had returned to Madagascar once, in 2001, to conduct a survey on my behalf of Midongy du Sud National Park in the southeast. It, too, was under consideration by UNESCO to become a World Heritage Site. Amanda and Miguel had traveled throughout the area on rough, unpaved roads, talking to people and estimating the infrastructure needed to raise the park to UNESCO's standards. But the area was so remote that the dossier was finally declined. Tourists would never be able to travel on the roads and building any infrastructure would be a challenge.

Miguel was subsequently hired by a Caribbean tourist enterprise, and Amanda moved with him to the small island of Culebra, off Puerto Rico. I would visit them there, a fourth destination along with Helsinki, Madagascar, and New York. Miguel worked as a dive master and eventually earned his captain's license, while Amanda worked for a tourist rental business. They both loved being on the water.

Amanda couldn't come to Madagascar for the inauguration of Centre ValBio because she was taking care of her first baby. She went into labor on Culebra, and needed to be evacuated to Puerto Rico for an emergency Cesarian section. Arianna Wright Poston was born on May 1, 2003. Miguel called me in New York to say baby and mother were fine. However, the grandmother was a wreck. I couldn't be sure everyone was okay until I saw for myself. I flew down to Puerto Rico. When I saw my granddaughter, it was love at first sight. Arianna had big brown eyes and long, dark lashes. The most beautiful baby I had ever seen . . . even more beautiful than a baby sifaka.

CHAPTER FOURTEEN

SAPPHIRE CITY

(2007)

OVER THE YEARS, I had directed many expeditions to Madagascar: teams of hardened researchers, eager graduate students, and inexperienced Earthwatch members. However, the one I led over Christmas 2007 was the most unusual because it was made up of fellow MacArthur "Genius" Grant Award–winners.

After winning the grant myself in 1989, I found I'd been inducted into a close-knit group of people in various fields through the arts to the sciences, who kept in close communication with each other and sometimes traveled together. So, on the trip I planned were Raphael Lee, a surgeon at the University of Chicago; Erik Winfree, a computer scientist from Cal Tech; Susan Kieffer, a geologist investigating Saturn's new moons; Bill Viola, an artist who set the standard for modern videography; Joan Abrahamson, a lawyer interested in social change; my old mentor, John Terborgh, the tropical biologist who directed Cocha Cashu where I studied owl monkeys; Mimi Koehl, a marine biologist at Cornell University; Paul

Richards, an English historian; Henry Wright, an archeologist; and Ingrid Daubechies and Karen Uhlenbeck, both mathematicians—as well as their spouses and children. This group kindly attended my ceremony at the University of Antananarivo where, wearing my academic robes and my two medals of honor, I received an honorary degree, which commemorated Centre ValBio and the UNESCO World Heritage Site status that Ranomafana National Park had attained as one of the rainforest parks in the Atsinanana World Heritage cluster.

Upon arriving at Ranomafana, the Fellows were amazed at what we'd managed to achieve at Centre ValBio and got to experience eight species of lemurs within Ranomafana National Park. I had an unexpected surprise for the MacArthur group. Larry Page and his bride Lucy Southworth arrived for a few days of seeing the forest on their honeymoon. The Pages flew to northern Madagascar and the MacArthur Fellows and I drove to Isalo National Park, the glorious land of sandstone formations and canyons, which I'd last visited in 1999. We stayed at the new Jardin du Roy Hotel, the twin hotel built by the same French family who'd hosted Amanda, Sarah, and me in 1999. Like the first hotel, the Jardin du Roy was a lovely establishment, which blended into the sandstone massif itself and contained stone mosaics, marble staircases, domed windows, and hardwood lintels. The MacArthur Fellows would appreciate the Malagasy batiks on the walls and the decorative animals woven out of raffia scattered throughout the main building.

Less than five miles from this hotel was Ilakaka, better known these days as Sapphire City, as it was the world's largest supplier of sapphires. By 2007, the population of three thousand people had swelled to 100,000. Makeshift houses had been replaced by cement structures, and although there were still casinos, bars, and bordellos, a mosque and two churches had also been established. Along the main street, National Highway #7, stores sold water pumps, wheelbarrows, televisions, cans of gas, pairs of shoes tied by their laces, and suitcases. The smells of dried fish, fried bananas, mango peels, and human sweat mixed together. Rap music blared, and neon signs blinked mixed signals for "saphirs" and "massage." The place was as dangerous as ever. Soldiers with machine guns sauntered along the streets past children carrying pails of water on poles or pushing carts filled with firewood. I would just have to make sure that the MacArthur Fellows, especially their children, didn't venture into Ilakaka.

As for myself, I definitely wanted to go there.

That October, while I was in Ranomafana, I'd heard that bones had been found in Ilakaka. The news came from a boy named Angelin, whose grandmother was Queen of Ambodriana, a region south of Ranomafana. This meant that Angelin himself would one day be king. When we'd last met him in 1991, Angelin was a bright, seventeen-year-old boy who helped us to assemble the Ranomafana Museum. He was particularly fascinated by bones and had helped Jukka catalog hippo subfossils that had been excavated from a streambed in Ampoza, just west of Isalo National Park. Angelin's dream was to someday visit the American Museum of Natural History in New York City, where there would be more bones than he could count.

"What kind of bones did you say were found?" I asked Angelin.

"Dinosaur bones."

I tried to hide the skeptical look on my face. Dinosaur bones would be an unusual find in the south of Madagascar, although they'd been discovered in the north. "And who found them?"

"My uncle's friend, Germaine. His crew was digging for sapphires along the Ilakaka River, fifty feet deep, when they hit a layer of smelly, slate-gray clay. The layer was filled with giant bones, and underneath them were sapphires. . . ."

I had stopped listening at "giant bones." "So what did Germaine do with the bones?"

"He put them into sacks and hid them because he was afraid that someone would steal them. He thinks they are valuable. Are they?" We had trained Angelin in the importance of documenting the context of where bones come from to be able to reconstruct what was going on when the animals were alive.

"Yes," I said. "Most likely they are. Thank you, Angelin. Are you going to be visiting your uncle anytime soon?"

It turned out that Angelin would be in Ilakaka with his extended family over Christmas, the same time I would be in Isalo National Park with the MacArthur Fellows. The timing couldn't have been better. I arranged to meet with him and his uncle on Christmas Eve.

In the meantime, I couldn't get these bones out of my mind. What had Angelin's uncle's friend Germaine really found fifty feet below the ground? Most fossils in Madagascar were on or just below the surface, or in limestone recesses like the Crocodile Caves in the north. These deep bones could belong to dinosaurs or giant lemurs, or were just a bunch of stones carved to look like dinosaur bones. Whatever they were, I intended to find out.

On the afternoon of Christmas Eve, Jukka and I and a few interested MacArthur Fellows visited Ilakaka. The town came into view as Tom, our driver, took us west down National Highway #7, tin roofs fanning out on either side of the road like the scales on a butterfly's wings. Resembling a sparkling jewel itself, Sapphire City at a distance reminded me of Las Vegas.

We turned onto an unpaved road off the highway, then left at a mosque, and stopped in front of a row of wooden shacks. Angelin was standing outside one of them to meet us. As we followed him up a flight of rickety stairs to his uncle's living room, a boom box blared the theme to *Star Wars*. Inside the stifling room were chairs arranged around a coffee table covered with a lace cloth and a vase containing a bouquet of pink plastic flowers.

Angelin introduced us to his uncle and aunt, as well as the prospector named Germaine, who'd originally found the bones. About forty years old, Germaine was dressed in dark blue sweatpants, a blue hoodie, and flip-flops. He spoke Malagasy with a sort of stutter, and at first only talked to Angelin. Angelin's uncle and aunt were quite social and spoke French to us. Perhaps forty, the aunt wore her hair in tight braids covered by a brimmed straw hat and showed three gold teeth when she smiled. I noticed she wore bright pink gemstone earrings and a matching necklace. When I complimented her on them, she told me that they were sapphires, which surprised me—I didn't know that sapphires came in a color other than blue.

Through Angelin, I said to Germaine, "We heard that you found some interesting bones recently."

"Yes, many bones."

"Is it possible to see them?"

Slowly, Germaine reached into his pocket, pulled out a white handkerchief, and spilled a handful of bones onto the coffee table, like dice. Jukka looked at each bone carefully.

"These are real bones, but not dinosaur bones," he said.

Angelin translated to Germaine, who frowned.

Jukka continued. "This is a hippo toe bone, and this is a leg bone of a tortoise, and this is the tooth of a crocodile. "And this. . . ." He took the last bone between his thumb and forefinger, holding it up to the light. "This is a part of an elephant bird's foot. Very interesting."

Germaine relaxed. He told us that the rest of the bones— the large ones—were hidden about an hour's drive from here. But he was afraid to show them to us. He didn't explain why. After some coaxing, he agreed to meet us at dawn the next morning. I smiled and stood up, ending the meeting, and we started down the stairs with the rain pounding on the tin roof like a drumbeat. Belatedly, I realized that I'd just agreed to go hunting bones on Christmas morning.

At 4 A.M. on Christmas Day, Jukka and I set out with Angelin and Germaine and a few MacArthur Fellows to the west of Ilakaka. Thankfully, the rain had stopped. The dirt road was banked at first by makeshift huts. Then, we passed onto the flat landscape of the sandy beige anthills, which we now knew were sapphire mines. After an hour, we passed over a ridge of sandstone mountains and through a valley to a town called Ilakakabe, south of Ilakaka. A Lutheran church towered over the 150 or so houses, and the cement stalls reserved for the market were quiet and empty this morning.

We stopped at a large fig tree south of this town, and Jukka and Germaine continued on foot to examine the hidden bags of bones at Ilakakabe. After half an hour they returned, and Jukka reported that there were more than ten gunnysacks filled with the bones of hippos, tortoises, elephant birds, and giant crocodiles—all extinct species in Madagascar. Many of these bones were over a foot long and heavy. I could understand why Germaine had mistaken them for dinosaurs. Although this was a substantial find, I was disappointed that there were no bones of the giant lemurs. Might there be some in the pit where Germaine had found them? I convinced him to take us there.

We drove thirty minutes more to the river, a ribbon of shimmering sunlight snaking through flat grassland, and got out of the car to walk the rest of the way. The sun had risen by now and the heat was starting to pound down. There were few trees to offer shade. As I passed by one tree, I startled as a branch appeared to move. Wrinkled eyes swiveled to focus on me, and I realized the branch was a foot-long chameleon. Further down, we encountered three women wearing braided hair and brightly colored *lambdas*, sorting through pebbles on a flat rock by the river. I saw homemade screens next to them and realized they were "panning" for sapphires. The banks were lined with layers of red, brown, and beige stones, as if laid by an ancient mason.

Then Jukka called out, "Look!" We climbed up the bank and he pointed at a round hole exactly the width of a human torso. I flicked my flashlight toward the hole and saw that it went straight down in a perfect circle for thirty feet. Germaine explained that this was the first step of a sapphire mine. If a miner found sapphires after digging down for thirty feet, he would tunnel to the sides. Apparently, this mine had been abandoned.

The place where Germaine had found the bones was directly across the river, hidden by mounds of dirt. The water was swift and waist-high, but we waded through. I could never have imagined what lay beyond those mounds, which were perched on the rim of an enormous pit, about thirty feet on one side and nearly four stories deep, with terraced clay walls that ended in a greenish pool of water. Once upon a time, the Malagasy hippopotamus had lived in the marshes near the river, emerging at night to graze. The giant crocodile, which could grow as long as sixteen feet, had preyed on them. The crocodile probably also hunted the elephant bird, the ten-foot-tall one called *Aepyornis* and the shorter, ostrich like *Mullerornis*. We had evidence from other sites (cut marks on the bones) that humans feasted on all these big fauna, probably causing their extinction. Giant lemur fossils found by Dr. Simons in a limestone cave about sixty miles north and west of where we were standing had been dated to 500 C.E., after the fall of the Roman Empire. I wondered how old these fossils were, so deep in the ground.

As we circled the pit, Germaine would reach down, pick up

tiny bits of bone, and offer them to me. I put them in my vest pockets and soon they were stuffed. Also on the ground were piles of small pink sapphires, similar to those that Angelin's aunt had worn, but I preferred the bones. Unfortunately, none of the bones appeared to have ancient lemur characteristics.

All too soon, we needed to head to the car. Jukka and I were supposed to get back to the hotel in time to have Christmas dinner with the MacArthur Fellows. But when we got to the village of Ilakakabe, two armed soldiers stopped the car.

"What's going on?" Jukka whispered to me.

I didn't know and shook my head. Under the soldiers' command, Tom drove us to the police station. He, Germaine, and Angelin were ordered inside for interrogation, while Jukka, the MacArthur Fellows, and I remained in the car. I noticed bullet holes in the station's front door and wondered what we'd gotten ourselves into. I knew that in Malagasy jails, cattle rustlers and murderers alike were put in a single cell and no food or toilet was provided. Sometimes prisoners were beaten.

After a while, Tom reappeared and said he needed to get our permits and other official papers from the glove compartment. His reassuring tone didn't hide the fact that he was terrified. Then he whispered to us that the Commandant of the Gendarmerie himself would be coming to speak with us. The police thought we were trafficking in the bones of the ancestors, a worse crime than committing murder in this region. No wonder Germaine had been scared. I regretted putting the bone fragments in my vest pockets, and hoped the police wouldn't decide to conduct a strip search. Visions of a lifetime spent locked up in a Malagasy prison danced in my head. Meanwhile, the MacArthur Fellows had no idea that there was a problem. Susan Kieffer was pointing out the moons that surrounded Saturn to Paul Richards. And Paul Richards was describing the cathedral music playing at Christmas in England.

After about half an hour, several gendarmes emerged from the station and motioned for Jukka and I to get out of the car. We did so with shaking knees.

Then the Commandant of the Gendarmerie arrived, disturbed from his Christmas dinner. I was terrified as he approached, guns at his sides.

"Madame Patricia!" he exclaimed. "Is that you?"

To my surprise, I recognized my friend the Commandant Ralivo from Ranomafana! He'd been transferred a few years ago—luckily for me, to Ilakakabe. I grinned my recognition.

Immediately, the Commandant began to bark at his underlings. "How could you think about arresting Madame Patricia? She has two medals of honor from the President. She built Ranomafana National Park." Then he turned to me. "Welcome to our humble village, Madame Patricia. You are most welcome here."

I explained that Jukka and I were interested in ancient animal bones, not human ones, and that our Malagasy friends were helping us with our work. With a wave of his hand, the Commandant had Tom, Germaine, and Angelin released from the police station. They were very glad to see us. Then, with a serious expression, the Commandant said that we'd need to get our bones "certified." I had no idea what that meant.

"You need to ask the doctor from the village to examine your bones and certify that they are not human," the Commandant explained. "I will summon the doctor and you can get your bones certified right now."

Together, we walked to the hut in the south of the village where Jukka had seen the bones at dawn. The adobe walls didn't contain any windows, but this hut housed unimaginable treasures: two tons of bones that Germaine had saved for almost two years in ten sacks. These sacks, as Jukka had observed earlier, were full of hippo, crocodile, and elephant bird bones. No lemurs.

Many of the villagers had followed us to the hut, and now they crowded outside, wanting to know what was going on. As if someone had turned on a television camera, Angelin was transformed into a talking head. As each bone emerged from the sack, he talked in Malagasy about what animal it belonged to. Jukka and I watched proudly as he told the rapt audience about the ancient beasts that lived in this neighborhood thousands of years ago.

He would still be there telling stories if my cell phone hadn't rung, breaking the spell. The Commandant told me that a cell tower in Ilakaka had been erected last month. I still wasn't used to this and other signs of modern technology making inroads into Madagascar.

The call was from Dede at the hotel, telling me that I was late for Christmas dinner. After dropping off Germaine and Angelin in Ilakaka, Tom drove us back to the Jardin du Roy, in time for Christmas dinner with the MacArthur Fellows.

CHAPTER FIFTEEN

NOTHING GOLD
CAN STAY

(2008)

AFTER RETURNING to the United States, I continued to wonder about the giant bones near Ilakaka. This subfossil site was the farthest east of any subfossil site in the south of Madagascar. In 1932, the French paleontologist Charles Lamberton found the last subfossil site in the south, on the west coast near Toliara. Because Lamberton had discovered hippos there, he'd called it Lamboharana, "the place where the pigs play in the water." This new site could provide very important information to what was known about Madagascar's subfossils. But if I wanted to go back there, I needed help. Only one person had the reputation and permits to go quickly to Madagascar and follow up on this discovery.

I dialed the number for Elwyn Simons at Duke University. "Elwyn," I said. "I have a problem. We've just discovered a new subfossil site, east of Isalo National Park." I explained that we'd found hippo, crocodile, turtle, and elephant bird bones.

"But no lemurs?" Elwyn cut to the chase.

"No lemurs yet. What intrigues me is that the deposits are fifty feet deep."

"*Hmmm*. None of the marsh sites are deep: Ampoza, Lamboharana, Ampasambazimba all have bone beds near the surface. The deeper the deposits, the older the sites could be and the more likely older lemur bones will be there." I could tell he was getting interested.

"So, will you go back there with me?" I asked, hopefully.

"Yes. But there's a problem with that. A big problem. Don't tell anyone." And Elwyn's voice went low, as if someone was listening in. "I need to get a hip replacement."

My heart sank. I knew Elwyn was getting older, but this was the first time that he sounded like he was slowing down.

"So I can't go right away," he continued, "but I should be ready in August." Sounding more like himself, he added, "There had better be subfossil lemurs at your new site, Wright!"

In August, the research team that Elwyn and I put together went to the subfossil site near Ilakaka. The members included Elwyn's right-hand man PJ; Angelin; Professor Armand Rasamimanana, Chair of the Department of Paleontology at University of Antananarivo; and two students, one of Armand's and one of Jukka's geology students from the University of Helsinki. Jukka was an invited speaker at a developmental biology conference this time and couldn't come.

Our questions were basic: What was the land like thousands of years ago? Were there any subfossil lemurs at this site? And how old were these bones? The crucial question had to do with the bones' age. If these bones were dated anywhere between a thousand and two thousand years ago, they wouldn't be very interesting to us. All the marsh subfossil sites had been dated in that time period, meaning this site would be very similar to all the others and not provide new information about the evolution of these animals.

However, because of the depth at which the bones were found, we hoped that these bones were older. If they were, then we could measure the changes of these creatures through time. If the species didn't change in size or shape, then we could surmise that the environment had been quite stable before humans arrived. If they were larger or smaller or different in any way, we'd have to figure out why these changes had occurred.

But before any research in Madagascar could proceed, diplomacy needed to be accomplished. Elwyn had research permits from the Malagasy government to excavate and study the fossils, so that wasn't a problem. But this site was difficult because of its proximity to Ilakaka. The people in this region were accustomed to getting top dollar for things that came out of the ground (like sapphires). Professor Armand, who'd been raised in Ivohibe, a region just east of Ilakaka, and from the Bara tribe, would be our ambassador.

When we arrived at the mayor of Ilakakabe's house, a group of children crowded around us. The mayor himself came to the door to greet us. His smile was engaging and he was much younger than I expected. He invited us into his living room, which was festive with filmy pink embroidered curtains and bouquets of roses on the tables. Elwyn removed our permits from his briefcase, and we started by talking about our professions and how many years we'd spent researching in Madagascar. I also recounted how I'd met Germaine and discovered the site the previous December.

Then the mayor spoke. "Tomorrow morning we will go visit the elder in the village next to the river. All the people that will dig for you must be from that village. Did you say you wanted fifteen people to dig for fifteen days? Each of these men will begin to work at 6 A.M. and end the work day at 4 P.M. They will leave the worksite for two hours for lunch. You will not provide them with lunch—they will eat rice at home. Who will be your foreman?"

I glanced at Elwyn. We hadn't discussed that. "Germaine?" I suggested.

"Make sure you decide what you will pay him. Don't pay him too much, but he must receive more than the diggers. The diggers will each receive 5,000 ariary a day: no more, no less. At the end, give them an extra day's wages as a tip. If you follow these guidelines, all will be fine."

I quickly figured out that each digger needed to receive $2.50 a day, which multiplied by fifteen meant $37.50 a day. That meant fifteen workers digging for fifteen days would cost $562.50, not counting Germaine's wages. This amount seemed reasonable and within our budget.

After settling where and when to meet the mayor the next day, I took Elwyn to the windowless hut in Ilakakabe where the ten sacks full of bones had been stored for two years, so that he could see the bones for himself. Jukka had determined that these bags of bones contained subfossils, but we had not quantified them by species a year ago.

Elwyn spread each sack's contents one at a time on a big blue tarpaulin, Tom, PJ, Dede, and he then sorted and counted each bone. "About half of them are crocodiles and tortoises," he said. "About a quarter are hippos, including some jaw and skull fragments. The rest belong to elephant birds."

"Any lemurs?" I had to ask.

Elwyn looked at me with a tiny smile in the corner of his mouth but said nothing.

Later, we joined the others at our lodgings at La Palme de l'Isalo Hotel near the Isalo Massif. This new hotel was south of the road that led to the famous tourist site called "La Fenêtre," a rock formation resembling a window. Many tourists would take photos of the sunset framed by sandstone. Just this past April a busload of Italian tourists had been held up at gunpoint on their way to this site, and a police station had recently been installed there to combat further crime. While a police presence hadn't always been welcomed by me in this region, I preferred it in the light of Ilakaka's dangerous reputation.

Even though we'd be staying in the hotel, we wouldn't be eating in its restaurant. Elwyn and PJ were in charge of this expedition, and this was their decree. As had been the custom for the past forty years they'd gone on expeditions together, the drivers cooked. That first night, the two drivers unloaded a forest-green plastic picnic table with attached benches. They peeled onions and boiled rice while the rest of us sat delicately on the picnic set sipping J&B Scotch whiskey.

As we waited for our rice and beans, Elwyn entertained us

with a story. "In the late 1800s, some French explorers got lost north of Toliara, in the limestone karst area. Not many people lived there, and the French were getting hungry. Some local people found them and took them home for some cassava. Then the local people told them about a cave where they'd found bones. The French paleontologists wanted to see these caves. They stayed on for months, mapping all the cave openings that the local people showed them. Then they left, never to return."

Elwyn raised his glass to Armand.

"Armand was the one who showed me those hand-drawn maps in L'Academie Malagache. About five years ago, I took those maps and I drove down to Toliara and I found the caves. Most of them didn't have any bones. Then I found an opening in the limestone. By holding onto a tree, I was able to balance over the hole and look into it. It was deep and my flashlight didn't throw light very far. I couldn't see a thing, but I had a hunch this place was full of bones.

"You know I'm a bit, well, should I say, stout? And PJ isn't much better, so we couldn't get down into that hole. We had to get youngsters like Tab Rasmussen to descend into those caves. Those guys are professional cavers, and they went down on ropes, to which they tied buckets and lowered them as well. At the bottom of this cave, which was called Ankelitelo, they found a pile of bones. Lemur bones, one upon the other. It looked like the lemurs had accidentally fallen into the hole. The cave was 300 feet deep so they didn't have a chance of surviving the fall. We found *Palaeopropithecus*, the giant sloth lemur as big as a German shepherd, and *Megaladapis*, as big as a chimpanzee. Tab and the other cavers hoisted the bones up in the buckets, and PJ and I just sat up there at the top of the hole and catalogued them as they arrived."

Elwyn took a big swig.

"And you know what? We dated those bones. Those are the youngest subfossil bones ever found. We got dates that were less than 500 years old. That's like yesterday in paleontology. Five hundred years ago, Columbus had already discovered America and Henry VII was King of England. If we'd been born then and gone to Madagascar, we could have seen those lemurs."

By this time, the rice and beans were cooked, and we started to eat. When we'd almost finished, Elwyn revealed the point of his story.

"After the mayor takes us to see the elder tomorrow, PJ and I are going to Ankelitelo. We found a nearly complete *Palaeopropithecus* skeleton there and a fine *Megaladapis* skull and we want to find more lemur bones at Ankelitelo."

"What?" I protested. "What about the site here?"

"You'll be fine," Elwyn assured me. "You and Armand can lead the expedition."

PJ chimed in. "Yesterday I was at the market and bought food for 15 days—bread, coffee, tea, canned milk, rice and beans, even fried locusts. There was a plague of locusts in the grasslands last week and the local children captured them to sell as snacks. They're good, you'll like them."

I shuddered. But it had been decided; Elwyn and PJ were going west, and the rest of us were stuck with two weeks' worth of fried locusts.

The next day, the mayor took us to meet the elder and his wife in their village, which consisted of ten adobe huts with thatched roofs.

After the introductions, the elder asked Elwyn, "How old are you?" This would be considered impolite in Western culture, but in Madagascar, age was status.

"I'm seventy-eight," Elwyn replied.

"I too am seventy-eight years old," said the elder. "In which month were you born?"

"July."

The elder broke out in a big smile. "I was born in April." He had won the "age game." The elder shook hands with Elwyn and led the way to the river for the ceremony.

This ceremony was attended by only our team, the mayor, and the village elders, but the zebu sacrifice that would take place the next day would involve over a hundred people, who would each take home their portion of meat. This public sharing assured that not only would we have good luck in finding fossils, but that we'd be spared from being robbed or sabotaged.

Before he left for Toliara, Elwyn whispered to me, "Yesterday I saw the jaw of a *Megaladapis—Megaladapis edwardsi* I think. Good luck." And he hoisted himself into the front seat of the car and gave a royal wave out the window as the vehicle headed south. So my hunch was correct: lemur bones had been found at our site.

As the new heads of the expedition, Armand and I began the process of choosing our workers. We ended up picking fifteen strong young men who represented each family living near our site. Germaine agreed to be our foreman, and he called roll each morning to make sure everyone was on time. At the end of each day I handed a 5,000 ariary note to each worker in front of the others for transparency. Although the ariary had been around since 1961, and was pegged at 1 ariary to 5 Malagasy francs, it had become the official currency only three years previously. The mayor had told us that the money would go toward dowries for the workers to get wives.

We were digging in the enormous pit Germaine had showed me last December, but it had filled in from the rainy season and we now were making it deeper and wider. Every day we loaded up the car with bottled water and food for the day. Tom would drive us from the hotel to the fig tree where the road ended, and we'd walk to the river. We sat on the riverbank, rolled up our pant legs, and took off our hiking boots. Slowly, we waded through the swift current, carrying our boots. The river bottom was mostly rounded pebbles and sand. On the other side, we slipped on our boots and followed a thin path along the river's edge to the pit where the workers waited. Most of us dug with them. Armand was especially interested in ammonites, an extinct kind of marine invertebrate similar to a squid. They were found in a geological formation called sakamena, named after a region in Madagascar. The sakamena formation had not been studied this far south before.

The first day, as I ate lunch under a tree, I reached down at its base and wedged into the roots was a bone fragment with three worn teeth. Instinctively, I knew it was a primate jaw. The shape of the teeth distinguished it from hippo teeth. Its pattern, like ribbon candy, suggested it belonged to *Megaladapis*, one of the largest of lemurs. There are few things more amazing than holding the jaw of an extinct primate in your hand: especially when you're the first to find it.

Armand came over, praised my keen eyesight, and confirmed my identification. "Probably *Megaladapis edwardsi*." Also called the koala lemur, this species weighed over a hundred pounds. It had a long cow like face with eyes on either side, and probably ate branches and leaves that it ripped off with its long nose, like a tapir does in the rainforests today. Its limb bones suggested it didn't move very fast.

Each day the pit got deeper, and the workers began to divide up with one team below at the deepest level, and the other team moving the dirt that the first team dug up. Our next big find happened three days later. One worker walked up with the vertebrae of a hippo. And less than a half hour later, that same worker triumphantly presented us with half a femur. It was small, and definitely not from a hippo.

"It's a primate femur." I turned the bone over in my hands. "Perfectly preserved."

Armand identified it as *Pachylemur insignis*, closely related to the present-day black-and-white ruffed lemur from the genus *Varecia*. "Look at that trochanter," he said, pointing to attachment for the leg bone. "Since *Varecia* eats fruit, this site must have had abundant fruit to support a population of *Pachylemur*."

The next two days proceeded with no bones, despite lots of digging. The men were terracing the site now, and different teams worked at different levels. We kept a careful eye on the deepest pit, waiting to see signs of the gray clay level, but all we saw was the color of sand.

On Day Five the workers handed up a thick bone the size of a dumbbell. The ends were damaged, but I could see by the porousness of the matrix that it was a bird bone.

"It's the thigh of an *Aepyornis*," Armand stated matter-of-factly. "Did you know that Prince Akishino, the brother of the crown prince of Japan, is interested in the elephant bird?"

We did not, so Armand explained that Prince Akishino was a scientist who'd written some very important papers on chicken genetics and the elephant bird. At least two species of extinct ratites lived here on Madagascar. Ratites are giant flightless birds like the living rheas from South America; ostriches from Africa, emus from Australia, and moas and kiwis from New Zealand. DNA studies had shown the closest relative to *Aepyornis* is the kiwi, despite the fact that the elephant bird species from Madagascar was bigger than any of those other ratites, and kiwis the smallest. *Aepyornis* was 10 feet tall and weighed over a thousand pounds. One egg was nearly the size of a dinner plate in circumference. The volume inside that egg was 160 times greater than that of a chicken's egg.

Prince Akishino had never found an egg in the center of Madagascar, as they were always in the sand dunes on the west coast, off the Mozambique Channel. He developed a theory that the adult birds must have migrated to the sea every year to lay and incubate their eggs. If they were like other ratites, the males would have sat on the nests, which have been found to hold as many as twelve eggs.

On Day Six I found the black jaw. Angelin and I were bone partners and spent every day walking around the huge mounds of earth on the rim of the pit, which had become hard and

crusted over since Germaine's crew had found the first bones
two years before. We used geology pickaxes to break the soil
to search for fragments. Angelin had sharp eyes, and we found
many crocodile jaws and lemur ribs. Just before we stopped for
lunch at the top of the easternmost midden, I saw teeth that
gleamed like obsidian in the sun. I picked up the jaw, realizing
with a flush of joy that it definitely belonged to a lemur. It had a
first molar and half of the second. Their ribbon-candy pattern
suggested another *Megaladapis*, but this jaw was heavier than
the other one I'd found and seemed to belong to an older time.

On Day Thirteen we hit the gray clay layer. But the water
was seeping in from the bottom of the pit as we dug below the
water table, and we didn't have a pump to keep the site dry.
We sent Tom to buy buckets and to find out how much a pump
cost. He came back with the news that a pump big enough
for this pit would cost a thousand dollars. I called Benjamin
Andriamihaja in Tana to ask about the possibility of borrow-
ing the money. He couldn't get us the money for over a week
(it was Saturday).

On the morning of Day Fourteen, the workers of the northeast wall of the pit hit something flat and an inch thick, maybe
a shell turned to stone. There was a lot of it, suggesting that it
belonged to several individuals. The water continued to seep
into the floor of the pit, and we needed six workers to bail it
out. By lunch, we had most of the tortoises excavated. Afterward, the clay layer expanded, and we found more hippo leg
bones. And then at 3:45 P.M. Armand called out to one of the
workers, "Be careful, look to the left wall!" The sand there
had begun to loosen and flake off. The worker rushed to col-

lect more tortoise bones, then leaped up to the next terrace. The part of the wall where he'd previously stood crumbled, covering the site where the tortoiseshell had been excavated a few minutes ago. I breathed a sigh of relief; it had been a mud slide, but small. Germaine called the end of the day.

The next morning, by the time we arrived at the site, the workers were digging but nervous, expecting a major cave-in soon.

They didn't have to wait long.

First, a pop like a firecracker, then a boom like thunder, and the north wall collapsed with a roar. The workers had seen it coming and had scrambled to safely. They stood above the pit, watching as all their labors were erased in an instant.

Finally, I said, "This is the end of the expedition." Our goal had been accomplished. We had found out where the bones had come from—forty-five feet down and ten thousand years ago.

It was a bittersweet moment. Silently, each worker collected his shovel and we walked back along the banks of the river. When it was time to wade across, I took off my boots and stepped into the water. On the other side of the river, I sat on the ground and put on one boot at a time. This was the very place the zebu had been sacrificed only two weeks before. I needed to tell the mayor of Ilakakabe that the expedition was completed for this year.

I briskly stood up and looked back at the expansive flat terrain that spread outward to the horizon. I gazed upon the vast openness, my vision blurred, and my mind traveled ten thousand years back in time.

I saw the river flow into a large shallow lake, much of it

reedy marshes. Around the edges of the marsh stretched green forests as far as the eye could see. Dozens of dark gray hippos floated in the lake, emitting grunts from their wide mouths. Giant crocodile eyes lurked beneath the surface of the water, waiting. Elephant birds as tall as giraffes plucked *Pandanus* fruits, as sweet as persimmons, from along the river.

In the forest, the giant lemurs fed on leaves and groomed each other. A long-armed sloth lemur with furry black ears and a beige face nursed an infant. Two young black koala lemurs play-wrestled on the forest floor. Four giant ruffed lemurs, a rich red color, huddled together for a nap. A group of nine black and white *Hadropithecus* jumped along the edge of the marsh.

The scene dazzled with life. But it was only in my mind. A fierce determination came over me. I couldn't let the bamboo lemurs, the silky sifakas, and the sportive lemurs go extinct the way the giant lemurs had. I knew then that I'd continue to fight for them the rest of my life.

EPILOGUE

On February 9, 2009, there was a coup d'état in Madagascar. In Antananarivo, huge fires erupted in the shopping malls, large crowds gathered on the Avenue of Independence, and the United States Embassy was invaded. President Marc Ravalomanana fled into exile in South Africa, and the new president, Andry Rajoelina, the thirty-four-year-old former disk jockey and mayor of Antananarivo, took office. The United States Embassy refused to acknowledge his leadership, and cut off all except humanitarian aid. The European Union followed suit soon afterward.

I was at Stony Brook when the coup occurred. By April the situation was so dangerous that I brought Benjamin Andriamihaja to Stony Brook for his safety. With all aid stopped to Madagascar, only the most intrepid researchers came to Centre ValBio. By this time we had 85 full-time staff members. Finances were desperate, but I didn't want to lay off our hardworking team. We decided that everyone would be on half salary until the political turmoil subsided. An additional 57 tourist guides in the village were now out of work, as tourists were canceling their vacations in Madagascar. I feared that Ranomafana National Park might never recover.

Not only was Ranomafana in danger, but the rest of the country's ecological systems were also threatened. President Ravalomanana became a conservation hero when in 2003 he'd vowed to increase the protected areas in Madagascar by three times and had accomplished this. The rates of deforestation throughout the country had not only slowed, but decreased from 2002 to 2008. Under his leadership the economy boomed, and by 2009 all the main roads were paved, international tourism was thriving, and the GNP was increasing by six to ten percent each year.

After 2009, under the new transition government, Madagascar became open to international thievery. Although in the 1980s timber had been sent to Europe, now Asian timber exploiters were beginning to cut rosewood in the protected regions in the north, including Masoala and Marojejy National Parks. In these timber exploitation areas, the bushmeat market was full of lemurs. In contrast, in Ranomafana our close relationship with local leaders gave us a strong position, and the timber exploiters were kept away.

To make things worse, that summer my personal life fell apart. After eighteen years of tricontinental romance, Jukka and I separated. Our closeness had always been reinforced by our work in Madagascar, so it seemed fitting that just as that country was collapsing, so was our marriage. At times, I wondered if it were worth it, this strange life as a scientist that required so much attention, making it difficult to hold together relationships.

When I told Amanda the news, she insisted that I come stay with her and her family, who now lived in the Virgin Islands. Amanda worked in the Marine Biology Department of the University of the Virgin Islands, and Miguel was the captain of a tourist boat. Six-year-old Arianna now had a brother, two-year-old Issan. There was no time to be sad with those two around. So with the support of Amanda and her family, and the turquoise waters of the Caribbean to remind me of the beauty of nature, I began the road to recovery. Within eight months, I began a closer relationship with colleague and friend Noel Rowe, the managing editor of "All the World's Primates" website/book project and president of Primate Conservation, Inc. Noel began to accompany me to Madagascar.

Meanwhile, the African Union insisted on free and fair elections for Madagascar in 2009, but the elections were officially postponed every six months, year after year. The international community continued to deny aid, and tourism greatly declined. The economy continued to plummet, and the illegal trade in timber reached unimaginable heights. But international flights resumed, and the researchers returned to Ranomafana by the end of the year, and we were able to pay full-time salaries again. As Ranomafana got back on its feet again, so did I.

In January 2010, the Herrnsteins, both astrophysicists trained at Harvard and now living at Stony Brook where Jim worked at Renaissance (a hedge fund), expressed an interest in the Ranomafana Project. They were looking for a venture in Africa where they could donate and also work with the local population. They visited Ranomafana and fell in love with the people, the lemurs, and the project. With their help, in 2012 we inaugurated a new four-story building with modern laboratories, spacious dormitories, a conference hall, computer room, and balconies for people to read and study outside. A "green building," it has solar panels to produce hot water, a green roof with gardens full of medicinal plants and herbs, a

rainwater recycling system, and an atrium system for airflow
and natural air conditioning. It is also a community center for
local arts, including music and handicrafts. We call this hall
NamanaBe, which means "big friendship"—the friendship
between wildlife and the people.

By 2013, Centre ValBio had been visited by over a hundred
researchers and tourism to the Ranomafana Park had risen to
23,000 tourists annually. Conservation was recovering and
NamanaBe Hall was a landmark accomplishment. During the
inauguration of the hall in 2012, I received a third medal—the
last of a series (Chevalier, Officier, and Commandeur) or Knight,
Officer, and Commander. Very few foreigners have received all
three, and it remains one of the greatest honors I have achieved
in my life. In 2014, I became Distinguished Professor and was
scientific advisor to the 3D IMAX film *Island of Lemurs: Madagascar*, narrated by Morgan Freeman with Dave Douglas as the
director and photographer and Drew Fellman as the producer.
The film features lemurs and my research. In September 2014, I
received the Indianapolis Prize, the "Nobel-like" award for Conservation, an extraordinary honor. In 1986, when I was worried
that the forests would all be destroyed and the golden and greater
bamboo lemurs would go extinct, I could never have imagined
that all these successes would occur one day.

In December 2013, I returned to Madagascar with Noel
Rowe and Amanda, Miguel, and Arianna and Issan, now
aged ten and six respectively. In Ranomafana, everyone was
delighted to see Amanda again and to meet her children. The
kids loved the rainforest. Amanda was amazed at the Centre ValBio's top-of-the-line laboratory, comfortable dorm

rooms, and hot showers. She always had a deep appreciation for architecture and it was gratifying for me that she found the building aesthetically pleasing as well as functional. And she loved the interior decoration, with Malagasy handicrafts and restored Malagasy furniture. We spoke about how the bamboo forest was expanding and how the places where the forest had been clearcut were now grown back. Amanda even mentioned how she'd noticed the economy of the region had improved with ecotourism and research salaries; although it was still poor, it wasn't desperately so. She was extremely proud that Emile, Loret, Dede, Pascal, Richard, and others had been able to build houses in Ranomafana, raise their families, send their children to high school and university, and live a middle-class lifestyle.

"Your dreams have really come true, Mom," Amanda told me, "although, we both know your work still isn't finished." I looked at her meaningfully, and put my arm around her. We'd just retraced the steps of our Isalo Ifaty trip and discovered that much of the unprotected forest in the region had been cut down and the coral reef was devastated. It had been very difficult for Amanda to see for herself the massive deforestation and the degradation of the reef.

The next morning, Loret and Emile made a special visit to take us all into Ranomafana National Park. While Amanda, Loret, and Emile caught up with each other's news, I showed Arianna and Issan around. They delighted being in my palace of green. Arianna enjoyed learning about the plants and Issan loved the reptiles, and even unexpectedly snatched up a snake. Thank God, nothing is poisonous in Madagascar!

I've received many awards and had successes beyond my wildest dreams, but none of them compare to the moment when I showed my grandchildren the golden bamboo lemur: safe, content, and the symbol of it all.

Ny tao-trano tsy vitan'irery. Only together can we save the lemurs and wildlife into the future.

ACKNOWLEDGMENTS

My daughter, Amanda Elizabeth Wright, allowed me to follow my dreams and still be a mother. I would like to thank her for loving lemurs, assisting me in following the sifakas, and giving me advice on delicately trudging through the politics of making a national park. I would also like to thank Elwyn Simons for encouraging me to go to Madagascar and for teaching me so much about fossils and life. Benjamin Andriamihaja has been a cheerful, wise, patient, and savvy partner through the politics of conservation in Madagascar. Madame Berthe Rakotosamimanana was a leader in forming Madagascar environmental policies and a fountain of wisdom and encouragement. Alison Jolly, Bob Sussman, Alison Richard, Ian Tattersall, Henry Wright, and Bob Dewar were pioneers who guided and advised me in those earliest years in Madagascar and thanks for their wisdom. Thanks to Robert Martin for his guidance on the description of the golden bamboo lemur. I appreciate our cooperation and partnership with the Madagascar National Park Service, the director general of MNP Guy Suzon Ramangason and the Ranomafana park managers—Mamy Rakotoarijoana and Josiane Rakotonirina. I am grateful to the Ministry of the Environment for giving us the permits and support to conduct research and for our programs in Madagascar.

Bill Arens, John Fleagle, Charlie Janson, and Lawrence

Martin convinced me to change universities from Duke to Stony Brook. Patrick Daniels devoted years of his life to helping make Ranomafana National Park a reality. Andrea Katz and I marched joyfully together through the early years at Duke. She and Charlie Welsh managed conservation efforts for Duke Primate Center and made the DUPC a joy for research. Emile Rajierison, Loret Rasabo, Georges Rakotonirina, Pierre Talata, Albert Telo, Richard Ramandrapihaona, and William Rakotonirina are thanked for being my first guides and advisors. Steve Zack taught me Malagasy birds, trained many Malagasy students, and gave me good advice. John Fleagle lent me support and kind encouragement along the bumpy road of navigating the park, the department, and our students. David Haring took excellent photos and has been a good friend through the years.

John Cadle is thanked for his intrepid exploration of Malagasy wildlife and research on frogs, chameleons, and snakes— and his friendship. Thanks to the biodiversity researchers who discovered new species and new ecology: Ron Altig (tadpoles), Ken Crieghton (rodents), Marian Dagosto (lemur locomotion), Helen Dixson and Julia Jones (crayfish), Luke Dollar (fossa), Louise Emmons (bats and carnivores), Beth Erhart (lemur ecology), Ny Hamashita (lemurs), Illka Hanski (dung beetles), Jukka Jernvall (lemur teeth), Lon and Myna Kightlinger (human parasites), Claire Kremen (butterflies), Jukka Lehtonen (mammals), Juha Laakonen (parasites), Jari Neimela (beetles), Bruce Patterson (water tenrecs), Rick Prumm (birds), David Quammen (biodiversity interactions), Peter Rienthal (fish), Mark-Oliver Rodel (frogs), Jim Ryan (red forest rats),

Mark Siddall (leeches), John Sparks (fish), Melanie Stiassny (fish), Suzanne Strait (lemurs), Miguel Vences (frogs), Chris Vineyard (lemurs), Jeff Wyatt (lemur viruses) and Steve Zack (birds). Remi Rakotosoa, Georges Rene Randriananirina, Laurent Randrianasolo, Telo Albert, and Raymond Ratsimbazafy are thanked for their loyal and persistant assistance and expertise with *Propithecus*.

Thanks to Duke University undergraduates Art Clemente, Alex Dehgan, Larry Dew, Mark Erdmann, Paul Ferraro, Amy Kemmerer-Nonnenmacher, Martin Kratt, April Pulley, Michael Todd, and Julie Deardorff, as well as Nigel Asquith, and Oliver Schwaner-Albright, who devoted their energy early on to make Ranomafana a national park. I appreciate all of the 500 undergraduates who have participated and been transformed by the Stony Brook Study Abroad program in Madagascar over the past twenty years and thanks to Bill Arens, Jen Green and Erin Achilles, Pat Paladines, and Tharcisse Ukizintambara for expediting the program.

My gratitude also to Chris and Maureen Chapple, my brother and sister-in-law, who encouraged their son Dylan to attend fall semester at Madagascar Study Abroad and who introduced me to Lantern Books (Dylan is now pursuing his PhD in environmental science, policy, and management at UC Berkeley); to Glenn Chapple, my brother and part-time soccer coach, who contributed the soccer balls for the villages; and to Eileen Scoville and Diane Woodhouse, my sisters, who rallied their schools to give donations to the park. Ted Chapple, my brother, gave his expert construction knowledge and wisdom for both Centre ValBio buildings, and advised me that

Ali Yapicioglu might understand the specialness of working in Madagascar. I'm grateful to Ali, Rick Hauser, and Peter Ozolins for their architectural expertise; their patience with a naïve, yet determined, client; and making the skeleton of a dream a fully fleshed-out reality. Mr. Lucien Robert and Mahefa, the contractor and engineer, worked on the ground through cyclones and complaints always remembering Centre ValBio would be built to last for a hundred years. I am grateful to the three directors of the Centre ValBio—Jean Phillippe Puyravaux, Anna Feistner, and Eileen Larney—for their extraordinary abilities to lead a fledgling and a complex research center.

To my graduate students, their students, and my post-docs, who with their keen observations and dissertations enhanced our knowledge of the lemurs and rainforests of Madagascar, and assured that science was energetic and fun: Summer Arrigo-Nelson, Andrea Baden, Elizabeth Balko, Matthew Banks, Liz Borda, Brenda Bradley, Kerry Brown, Santiago Cassalett, Tara Clarke, Kate Clark-Schmidt, Alex Dehgan, Amy Dunham, Debi Durham, Brian Gerber, Ben Greene, Sharon Gursky, Kim Hecksher, James Herrera, Christopher Holmes, Mitchell Irwin, Rachel Jacobs, Steig Johnson, Caitlin Karanewsky, Sarah Karpanty, Steven King, Elise Lauterbur, Sara Martin, Mireya Mayor, Adina Merelender, David Meyers, Toni Lyn Morelli, Jean Aimee Norosoarinaivo, Deborah Overdorff, Lisa Paciulli, Sharon Pochron, Leila Porter, Pascal Rabeson, Andry Herman Rafalinirina, Andry Rakotonavalona, Felix Ratelolahy, Jonah Ratsimbazafy, Jean Claude Razafimahaimodison, Onja Razafindratsima, Gena Sbeglia, Elizabeth Sperling, Pablo Stevenson,

Chia Tan, Stacey Tecot, Lydia Tongasoa, Andrew Zamora, and Sarah Zohdy. I am especially proud of Jonah Ratsimbazafy, who after receiving a PhD at Stony Brook, is now a leading conservationist in Madagascar. Bernhard Meier enlivened our lives at Ranomafana and then moved on to the north of Madagascar to rediscover *Allocebus*, the bushy-eared mouse lemur.

To our Centre ValBio staff, all eighty-five of them—but especially the lemur technicians and staff members Prisca Andriambinitsoa, executive staff assistant; Désiré Randrianarisata, head of logistics and audiovisual; Jean Claude Razafimahaimodison, head of TEAM; Pascal Rabeson, head of monitoring and partnerships; and Florent Ravoavy, head of conservation education. We couldn't have made this project a reality without our whole Centre ValBio family working hard together through thick and thin.

To the MICET staff, headed by Benjamin Andriamihaja, and including Benjy Randrianambina, Tiana Razafindratsita, and Jean Rakotoarison, and Tom Rakotomalala, for their hard work in making the logistics, permits, and politics of this project a success.

To the Stony Brook ICTE team including Rickie van Berkum, David Lowe, Lauren Block DoNOVAn, Cornelia Seiffert, Erin Achilles, and especially Patricia Paladines. Without the home team we wouldn't have been able make things happen in Madagascar or at Stony Brook. To Brian Woods, Dexter Bailey, and Mireya Mayor for their fundraising skills. To the administration of Stony Brook—the late Dr. John Marberger, Dr. Gail Habicht, Dr. Dennis Assanis, Bill Arens, and Presidents Shirley Kenny and Sam Stanley Jr.—for their support and visits to Ranomafana. I am also grateful to the University of Helsinki administrators, President Kari Raivio and Jari Neimela, who were instrumental in making this dream a real building.

To Blue McGruder, who inspired Earthwatchers, and who made it possible for my daughter Amanda to meet her husband Miguel.

Thanks to the National Geographic Committee for Research and Exploration, and NGS Conservation Trust—led by Peter Raven and John Francis, and including Scott Edwards, Nancy Knowlton, Stuart Pimm, Phil Gingerich, Tom Lovejoy, and other committee members—for being close friends and for their visit to Ranomafana in 2006.

To the many donors to the project, including Laura Lee Stearns; Susan and Stefan Findel; Roger and Rosemary Enrico; Jim and Robin Herrnstein; Lisa, Robert, Alex and Julia Lourie; Nancy Rapoza; Andy Sabin; Jim and Marilyn Simons; Cindy and Cassiday Horn; the Binnie Family, the Child and Tree Foundation, the John D and Catherine T. MacArthur Foundation; Liz Claiborne and Art Ortenberg Foundation; the Earthwatch Institute; Wenner-Gren Foundation; the Leakey Foundation; the Nando Perretti Foundation; the UNESCO World Heritage Fund; USAID; National Science Foundation, USA; National Institutes of Health, USA; the University of Helsinki; Conservation International; UNICEF, the Margot Marsh Biodiversity Fund; Primate Conservation, Inc.; IUCN Primate Action Fund; Laura Lee Stearns Douroucouli Foundation; Fulbright Fellowship Program; Man in the Biosphere Program; Chicago Zoological Foundation; TEAM, Seneca

Park Zoo, the Woodland Park Zookeepers Association, and Duke University Research Fund.

For their pioneering work in development around the park, I would like to acknowledge Dennis Del Castillo, Mark Fenn, Joe and Dai Peters, Pedro Sanchez, and Norman Uphoff.

I am very grateful to the Centre ValBio Advisory Board, including Jim and Robin Herrnstein, Joan Abrahamson, John Allman, Jonathan Aronson, James Brumm, Rhett Butler, Tom Gillespie, Steig Johnson, Mark Krasnow, Tom Lovejoy, Stuart Pimm, Wai Poc, Noel Rowe, and Barbara Wold.

Many thanks to David Douglas and Drew Fellman for inviting me to be scientific advisor on the IMAX film *Island of Lemurs: Madagascar*. To Michael Crowther, the Indianapolis Zoological Society, the Eli Lilly Company, Cummins Inc. and the committees that elected me the Indianaplois Prize Winner for 2014.

To Jukka Jernvall for those seventeen years of being chief advisor and collaborator on the politics, strategies, and science of Ranomafana National Park and Centre ValBio.

To Noel Rowe who loves primates and has devoted his life to helping other people study and protect them. And to all my friends and colleagues who helped make Ranomafana National Park and my lemur-filled life possible.

For helping with earlier versions of the manuscript I thank Rachel Ryan, Hazel Wodehouse, and Jukka Jernvall; and for the more final versions, Wendy Lee, Mireya Mayor, Amanda Wright Poston, and Noel Rowe. I would also like to thank the team at Lantern Books, including Martin Rowe, Kara Davis, and Gene Gollogly for their work on both of my memoirs.

ANIMAL SPECIES AND GENERA

aye-aye	*Daubentonia madagascariensis*
big-nosed chameleon	*Calumma nasuta*
black-and-white ruffed lemur	*Varecia variegata*
brown lemur	*Eulemur fulvus rufus*
collared lemur	*Eulemur collaris*
crested drongo	*Dicrurus forficatus*
crested ibis	*Lophotibis cristata*
diademed sifaka	*Propithecus diadema*
dwarf lemur	Cheirogaleus
eastern lesser bamboo lemur	*Hapalemur griseus*
Egyptian monkey	*Aegyptopithecus*
elegant Madagascar frog	*Mantidactylus elegans*
elephant bird	*Mullerornis*
elephant bird	*Aepyornis*
elephant-eared chameleon	*Calumma brevicornis*
falanouc	*Eupleres goudotii*
fat-tailed dwarf lemur	*Cheirogaleus medius*
fossa	*Cryptoprocta ferox*
fossil primate genus	*Ramapithecus*
giant crocodile	*Voay robustus*
giant lemur (extinct)	*Archaeoindris*

giant lemur (extinct)	*Pachylemur insignis*
golden bamboo lemur	*Hapalemur aureus*
gray-headed brown lemur	*Eulemur cinericeps*
greater bamboo lemur	*Hapalemur simus / Prolemur simus*
harrier hawk	*Polyboroides radiatus*
Henst's goshawk	*Accipiter henstii*
howler monkey	*Alouatta monotypic*
indri	*Indri indri*
koala lemur	*Megaladapis edwardsi*
langur monkey	*Semnopithecus entellus*
lemur (extinct)	*Archaeolemur*
lemur (extinct)	*Megaladapis madagascariensis*
lemur (extinct)	*Hadropithecus*
lemur genus	*Varecia*
Madagascar flufftail	*Sarothrura insularis*
Malachite kingfisher	*Alcedo cristata*
medium-sized lemur (extinct)	*Babakotia radofilai*
Milne-Edwards' sifaka	*Propithecus edwardsi*
missing link between monkeys and lemurs	*Afrotarsius*
mouse lemur	*Microcebus*
O'Shaughnessy's chameleon	*Calumma oshaughnessy*
owl monkey	*Aotus*
Perrier's sifaka	*Propithecus perrieri*

Philippine's tarsier	*Carlito syrichta*
rainbow fish	*Bedotia ranomafanensis*
red owl	*Tyto soumagnei*
red ruffed lemur	*Varecia rubra*
red-bellied lemur	*Eulemur rubriventer*
red-fronted brown lemur	*Eulemur fulvus rufus*
red-tailed vanga	*Calicalicus madagascariensis*
ring-tailed lemur	*Lemur catta*
screw pine	*Pandanus*
silky sifaka	*Propithecus candidus*
slender loris	*Loris tardigradus*
sloth lemur (extinct)	*Palaeopropithecus*
sportive lemur	*Lepilemur*
trondo mainty	*Ptychochromoides betsileanus*
vanga shrikes (family name)	*Vangidae*
Verreaux's (or white) sifaka	*Propithecus verreauxi*
white-collared brown lemur	*Eulemur fulvus albocollaris*
white-footed sportive lemur	*Lepilemur leucopus*
white-fronted brown lemur	*Eulemur fulvus albifrons*
woolly lemur	*Avahi*
zebu	*Bos primigenius*
Wright's sportive lemur	*Lepilemur wrightae*

ABOUT THE PUBLISHER

LANTERN BOOKS was founded in 1999 on the principle of living with a greater depth and commitment to the preservation of the natural world. In addition to publishing books on animal advocacy, vegetarianism, religion, and environmentalism, Lantern is dedicated to printing books in the United States on recycled paper and saving resources in day-to-day operations. Lantern is honored to be a recipient of the highest standard in environmentally responsible publishing from the Green Press Initiative.

www.lanternbooks.com